PRICE IS WHAT YOU PA... ...T.

A CHAIN OF FOLLY WILL ALWAYS END BADLY.

LIVE BENEATH YOUR MEANS.

GREAT LEADERS ARE GREAT TEACHERS.

BETTING ON TORTOISES CAN
CREATE LONG-LASTING WEALTH.

ORWELLIAN SHENANIGANS CAN TIP US
OFF TO FINANCIAL SHENANIGANS.

WHAT LOOKS SAFE MAY BE UNSAFE:
CHALLENGE ASSUMPTIONS AND BE OPEN TO NEW FACTS.

BEWARE OF GEEKS BEARING FORMULAS.

INVEST WITH CEOS WHO EXPLAIN IMPORTANT RISKS.

REMEMBER THAT LARGE, UNFATHOMABLE DERIVATIVES
ARE STILL FINANCIAL WEAPONS OF MASS DESTRUCTION.

INDECIPHERABLE DISCLOSURES TELL US
WHICH EMPERORS ARE NAKED.

RECOVERY DEPENDS ON CHOOSING TO RESTORE OUR
SOCIAL COMPACT AND TO RESET OUR MORAL COMPASSES.

THEY FOUGHT FOR SELF-EVIDENT TRUTHS.

Praise for *Buffett's Bites*

In turbulent times, Buffett's wisdom and Rittenhouse's tips are needed more than ever.

Thankfully, Mr. Buffett's trust in Rittenhouse lets her share this delightful book with us. I have worked with hundreds of organizations on governance, risk, and compliance initiatives, and he is right: moral courage and principles are essential to business sustainability and growth.

Buffett's Bites is a superb distillation of Buffett wisdom. Truly nourishing. L. J. Rittenhouse has done it again!

Buffett's Bites reveals the secret of Berkshire Hathaway's success: Buffett's disciplined capital allocation, liquidity management, and the work ethics of his managers.

L. J. Rittenhouse clearly and concisely shows us how to follow Warren Buffett's honest investment advice. *Buffett's Bites* is a must read now. It will be a valuable guide for years to come.

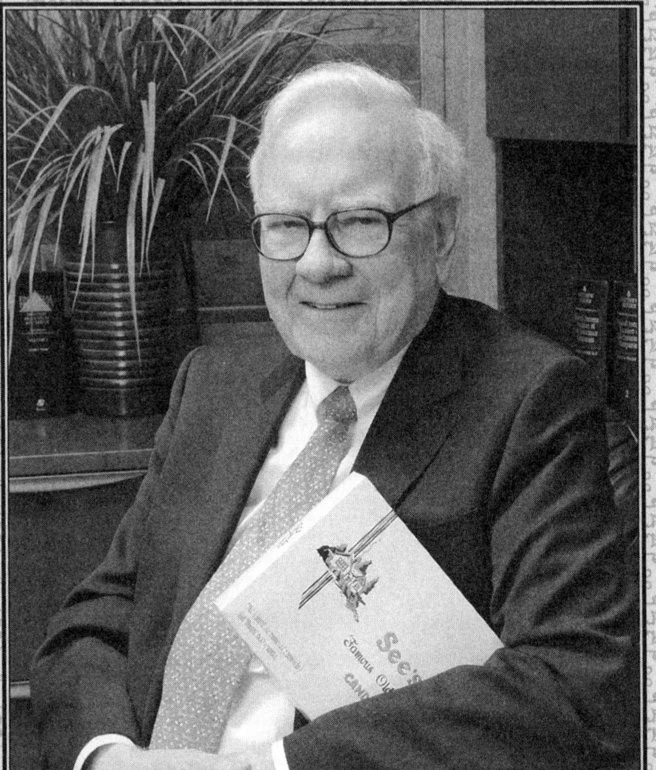
See's

BUFFETT'S BITES

THE ESSENTIAL INVESTOR'S GUIDE TO WARREN BUFFETT'S SHAREHOLDER LETTERS

L.J. RITTENHOUSE

New York   Chicago   San Francisco
Lisbon   London   Madrid   Mexico City   Milan
New Delhi   San Juan   Seoul   Singapore
Sydney   Toronto

The McGraw·Hill Companies

Copyright ©2010 by L. J. Rittenhouse. All rights reserved. Printed in the United States of America. Except as permitted under the United States Copyright Act of 1976, no part of this publication may be reproduced or distributed in any form or by any means, or stored in a data base or retrieval system, without the prior written permission of the publisher.

1 2 3 4 5 6 7 8 9 0   DOC/DOC   1 5 4 3 2 1 0

ISBN 978-0-07-173932-0
MHID   0-07-173932-7

Design by Lee Fukui and Mauna Eichner

This publication is designed to provide accurate and authoritative information in regard to the subject matter covered. It is sold with the understanding that neither the author nor the publisher is engaged in rendering legal, accounting, or other professional service. If legal advice or other expert assistance is required, the services of a competent professional person should be sought.

> —*From a Declaration of Principles jointly adopted*
> *by a Committee of the American Bar*
> *Association and a Committee of Publishers*

Copyright material is reprinted with permission.

The interior shot of shareholders coming down the escalator (page 78) and the exterior shot of the Qwest Center (page 164) are printed with the permission of Jeff Matthews, author of *Pilgrimage to Warren Buffett's Omaha* (2009), the definitive account of the Berkshire Hathaway shareholder meeting experience.

Frontispiece and head shots of Mr. Buffett on chapter openers © Jeff Lonowski.

Head shots of Mr. Buffett on part titles and page 8 photo © Getty photos.

McGraw-Hill books are available at special quantity discounts to use as premiums and sales promotions, or for use in corporate training programs. To contact a representative please e-mail us at bulksales@mcgraw-hill.com.

This book is printed on acid-free paper.

Contents

PART I
The ABCs of CEO Shareholder Letters

PART II
Bite-Sized Investor Truths

PART III
Principles-Based Capitalism for the Twenty-First Century

Preface

On Saturday, February 28, 2009, tens of thousands of people downloaded Warren Buffett's shareholder letter from the Berkshire Hathaway Web site. They were looking for investing tips. In their hurry to find real, not fool's, gold, many missed the best part of the letter: his principles. This is their loss. Following those principles, Buffett had bought Berkshire Hathaway, a struggling textile manufacturer, and turned it into one of the most respected companies in the world.

A lot of pundits didn't seem to "get it" either. Out of the 12,335 words in Buffett's 2008 letter, they quoted only six: *"the economy will be in shambles."* There was just one problem: The pundits dropped the end of his sentence: *"but that conclusion does not tell us whether the stock market will rise or fall."*

This six-word sound bite from the Oracle of Omaha spread throughout the media and blogosphere like a plague.

Markets tumbled. By the close of business on Monday, March 2, 2009, two days after Buffett released his letter, the S&P 500 Index had fallen to its lowest level since 1996. Can we bláme the pundits for this market drop? We will never know for certain. Still, why would responsible adults selectively quote a terror-inspiring phrase while the market was in free fall?

What can investors learn from this episode? Simple: "Ignore sound bites that rattle markets." It is one of 25 nuggets of wisdom—"Buffett bites"—extracted from his 2008 shareholder letter. Each bite offers a moral for turbulent times. I compare these nuggets of wisdom to chocolates in a box of See's candy. Both nourish us and give us pleasure; they can startle us, too. Who hasn't bitten into a chocolate candy expecting a caramel inside and found praline nougat instead? So it is with the Buffett bites. To get their full import, we must dig deeply inside.

Buffett's 45-year record of wealth creation at Berkshire Hathaway can't be beat. Buffett's bites, gleaned from his exemplary letters to shareholders, underscore the importance of his investing principles. If this small guide helps you to more clearly see the breadth of his principles for better investing and living, it will have succeeded.

For more than 12 years, I have used my Wall Street training to study Buffett's shareholder letters. What I learned led me to invent a discipline that measures the amount of candor in CEO communications. I became an executive candor expert. Each year, my business conducts an annual survey of CEO candor that shows how, on average, companies ranked highest in candor outperform companies ranked lowest. In addition, my research diagnoses the health of the underlying corporate culture, thus providing a clue to the trustworthiness of corporate accounting.

Buffett's Bites is my second project with Warren Buffett. The first occurred in the aftermath of Enron's collapse and 9/11. In early 2002, Buffett gave me permission to quote from his shareholder letters to write *Do Business with People You Can Tru$t*. It was released at the 2002 shareholder meeting in Omaha. Years later, knowing how protective he is of his words, I asked why he gave me a license to use them. Buffett said, "I trusted you." Buffett again has given me permission to quote from his letters for this book.

Perhaps one day more investors will notice what is now abundantly clear to me. The key to Berkshire's success is simple: Buffett practices the golden rule. He treats investors the way he would like to be treated; he tells them what he would want to know if he were in their shoes. If CEOs and boards of directors had followed his example in the past, many of us would be richer today.

Why not create a gold standard for CEO candor now? We can start by expecting it and looking for it. Investors with large holdings and important fiduciary responsibilities could make a huge contribution in this fight for clarity. They can start by holding CEOs accountable for giving us real, not phony, words. If we expect these investing professionals to raise the executive candor bar, it will be done.

These tasty Buffett's bites will help to point the way.

Introduction

The Buffett Mystique

What is right about the American dream? It inspires us to believe in a nation in which a small boy can collect bottle caps, sell used golf balls, deliver newspapers (and later in life join the board of the same paper), see his father exchange a grocer's apron for a stockbroker's tie, and then, far from Wall Street, become the greatest investor of his time.

Warren Buffett is ranked among the richest men in the world. The company he built, Berkshire Hathaway, has outperformed the S&P 500 for 38 out of 45 years. This feat alone qualifies him for the *Guinness Book of World Records*. Early investors in the company, including family and friends, have seen their Berkshire shares appreciate by 801,516 percent, or a 22 percent compounded annual increase versus just 9.3 percent for the S&P 500. Many with sizable holdings are now billionaires.

Every year since 1971, CEO Buffett has written a letter to his shareholders. Buffett writes the longest, most informative, and most entertaining letter of any CEO in the world. Unlike other executives, Buffett spends months polishing his prose and searching for the precise word needed to focus a thought. His goal is simple: to honor his words and keep his word. He wants to give his investors the information he would like to know if he were in their place.

A Capitalist, but Not a Materialist

In 2009, more than 35,000 people came to the Berkshire Hathaway annual meeting. They arrived hoping to catch a glimpse of the man with the Midas touch. Some hoped to snatch an autograph. In a six-hour Q&A-a-thon, Berkshire investors sat in a dark auditorium and watched Buffett and Berkshire Vice Chair Charlie Munger field investor questions. These ranged from seeking life advice to divining the direction of the economy. As in years past, the dialogue was informative and provided some of the best entertainment on the planet.

I've attended every shareholder meeting since 1997. Each year I talk with first-timers who have come to know Buffett through reading his annual shareholder letters. They arrive in Omaha curious to know whether the man they see at the meeting resembles the man they see in his communications. Are his letters real or fake? Does he live by his principles or merely talk about them? Does he keep his word? Buffett intrigues them because he is a capitalist, but not a materialist. He still lives in the house he bought back in 1950.

Buffett's compensation policy is simply stated in the Berkshire Hathaway proxy: "Mr. Buffett's annual compensation has been $100,000 for over the last 25 years, and he would not expect or desire it to increase in the future." He wants to make money for his investors, not off of them.

His influence goes beyond the business world. Journalist Thomas Friedman bases his foreign policy beliefs on what he calls "The Warren Buffett principle."* Buffett

---

* Op Ed column, *New York Times*, December 1, 2009.

works long hours to grow wealth for Berkshire shareholders, and why not? The bulk of his net worth is tied up in Berkshire stock. Still, Buffett credits his amazing success to one simple fact: He was lucky enough to have been born in America to parents who fed him, clothed him, and got him a good education so he could take advantage of American-grown opportunities. Buffett calls his good fortune the "ovarian lottery." Friedman writes that Buffett believes that "the primary obligation of our generation is to turn over a similar America to our kids."

In 2006, Buffett stunned the world when he announced that he would give his fortune, then valued at about $31 billion, to the Bill & Melinda Gates Foundation, to support initiatives that help the world's poorest people. He didn't ask to have a building named after him. The only strings attached to his gift are ones designed to ensure that the money is spent efficiently and gets to people who need it most.

This book is about Warren Buffett's shareholder letter, the mother of all CEO communications. It is about the quality of authentic leadership revealed by the words leaders use and the actions they take to honor their word. It is about the crisis of leadership we face at a time when we desperately need principled, responsible leaders. Buffett's shareholder letters stand out because of their clarity and rich vocabulary. He uses his genius with words to simplify complex issues and build trust.

Never forget that the United States was founded on honest words—beautiful ones like "life," "liberty," and the "pursuit of happiness." Our revolution was won by pistols and eloquence. *Common Sense*, Thomas Paine's fiery pamphlet released in January 1776, is still considered by historians to be the most widely read publication in American history. Paine's reflections on "these times that try men's souls" rallied thousands of patriots to abandon their farms for battlefields. Without Paine's words, there likely would have been no Revolutionary War.

Too few of our business leaders today use words that have the power and substance to restore our economy and this nation to greatness. Their leadership failure extends beyond the failure to make good on their promises. Their promises are flawed: They are small and serve narrow, limited interests. Instead of a fair deal, too often they give us a rigged deal. Buffett's shareholder letters prove that we should expect more from our leaders.

At the same time, while many people know that Buffett's greatness is revealed in his letters, fewer people actually read them. The number of Internet "hits" related to Buffett's modest home in Omaha exceeds the "hits" for his shareholder letters by 8:1.

Buffett's Bites: The Essential Investor's Guide to Warren Buffett's Shareholder Letters closes this gap by showing you how to spot CEOs who practice what Buffett preaches. Much can be gained from comparing Buffett's letters to those of other CEOs. By applying your critical reading skills to discern who is giving you real, not fool's, gold, you may become a richer investor, a smarter employee, a more effective job seeker, a more highly motivating leader, and a savvier customer and citizen activist.

The ABCs of CEO Shareholder Letters

What Are Shareholder Letters and Who Reads Them?

> Q: *Why doesn't Berkshire print glossy pictures in its*
> *annual report?*
>
> A. *There are no pictures that would aid in*
> *understanding Berkshire, but 10,000 words*
> *will—if they are carefully chosen.*
>
> —2002 INTERVIEW WITH WARREN BUFFETT

Every year legions of employees and paid consultants at thousands of publicly traded corporations around the world spend significant money and time to publish a letter from the CEO in the company's annual report. Occasionally the company's board chair and chief financial officer also contribute letters. These communications update investors on the company's results, reset the company vision, report key events, and offer an outlook on the future. For many investors, this communication is the only contact they have with a CEO.

I work with CEOs who write the first drafts of their shareholder letters. I know other CEOs who "author" their shareholder letters by contributing ideas and setting direction. This may not be a bad approach. Some people, including CEOs, are not gifted writers; and knowing what they can and cannot do well is a critical leadership skill.

But a third group of CEOs contribute very little to the writing process. Some executives in this ineffective group are "missing in action," while others add meaningless content. They sign their names to virtually incomprehensible shareholder letters. Too often I fear these same leaders are also missing in action when it comes to investing investor capital.

Remember that although these annual CEO updates are called "letters to shareholders," they are also read by employees (many of whom are shareholders), customers, partners, suppliers, journalists, legislators, and regulators, as well as shareholders. While some companies address their letters "To Our Stakeholders" or "To Our Investors, Employees, Customers, and Friends," most companies choose the conventional "To Our Shareholders."

But the salutation "To Our Shareholders" ignores an embarrassing reality. Most investors ignore them. Many say they aren't worth the paper they are written on. In fact, the shareholder letters in my annual surveys are loaded with massive amounts of PR spin and obfuscation. Still other investors complain, "Why bother? The CEO doesn't even write the letter."

More distressing is the untimeliness of these letters. Not long ago, the average holding period for stocks was about three years. Today it is about nine months. So why *would* the average investor read shareholder letters? He or she is out of the stock in less than a year.

You may ask, Why call these short-term stock pickers "shareholders" or "shareowners"? Isn't it more accurate to call them "stock renters," "stock flippers," or "traders"? These are valid questions. Remember, Buffett expects his Berkshire investors *never* to sell their stock. In the Berkshire Hathaway Owner's Manual, a codification of shareholder principles, he reminds them:

Charlie and I hope that you do not think of yourself as merely owning a piece of paper whose price wiggles around daily and that is a candidate for sale when some economic or political event makes you nervous. We hope you instead visualize yourself as a part owner of a business that you expect to stay with indefinitely, much as you might if you owned a farm or apartment house in partnership with members of your family. For our part, we do not view Berkshire shareholders as faceless members of an ever-shifting crowd, but rather as co-venturers who have entrusted their funds to us for what may well turn out to be the remainder of their lives.

In this book, the word "investor" refers to people and institutions that hold stocks for at least a year. The term "stock flippers" describes traders. If you rely on advice from a financial expert, you should ask if the expert is a trader or speculator or someone who invests in great, wealth-creating businesses.

Buffett follows a buy-and-hold strategy. He knows that building shareholder wealth takes years of patient, unstinting work. CEOs must put capital to work in ventures that need to mature, like good wine, before they can fully pay off and earn consistent, competitive returns. That's why investors need to know if the CEOs they invest with can be trusted to put their money to work in smart, productive ways.

Owner-Manager Capitalism

Since 1957, Buffett has written letters to partners and investors to explore his theories of owner-manager capitalism. He practices the golden rule of investor relations: Tell investors what you would want to hear if you were in their place. And he expects the same from the CEOs with whom he invests.

When I first read Buffett's shareholder letter in 1996, I was shocked to find his letter both hilarious and informative. It was personal. Today I expect the CEOs of companies in which I invest to provide the same kind of candid and authentic disclosure that Buffett offers. Why wouldn't every investor demand this? Long-term investors, such as pension fund managers, tell me that they keep five years of company annual reports on file. This allows them to evaluate the consistency of the CEO's messages over time and to track how accounting numbers are readjusted.

Never forget that a shareholder letter reveals the strength or weakness of the leadership and the corporate culture. Just as each person has a unique thumbprint, each company has a corporate thumbprint that differentiates it from all others. A really good shareholder letter reveals the detailed design of that thumbprint.

Why Read Shareholder Letters?

Although our form is corporate, our attitude is partnership.... Charlie Munger and I think of our shareholders as owner-partners, and of ourselves as managing partners. (Because of the size of our shareholdings we are also, for better or worse, controlling partners.) We do not view the company itself as the ultimate owner of our business assets but instead view the company as a conduit through which our shareholders own the assets.

—BERKSHIRE HATHAWAY OWNER'S MANUAL, PRINCIPLE 1

Most people read shareholder letters in the annual report expecting to get (1) a summary of the key events of the past year; (2) a report about the company's results in a meaningful context, and (3) an outlook for the year or years ahead. But letters can provide a great deal more. They offer an insider's view of the quality of leadership and the corporate culture.

What defines the Berkshire culture? Buffett makes it clear in the Owner's Manual: The culture at Berkshire is defined by an unflinching attitude of partnership. Buffett calls himself and Vice Chair Charlie Munger Berkshire's "managing partners." He regards Berkshire investors as the "owner-partners." This partnership perspective not only determines the style and content of Buffett's shareholder letters but also shapes his capital allocation decisions.

Leadership Quality and Stock Price

How important are CEO attitudes in determining the value of their company stocks? Various researchers and corporate consultants have estimated that investor perceptions of the CEO account for 40 to 60 percent of the stock price valuation—an impressive number.

In 1991 I left my Wall Street investment banking career to start an investor relations practice. My mission seemed simple. I would advise CEOs on how to shift negative perceptions to positive ones. I knew that their investors didn't want to get grandiose, generic, and obfuscating communications. They wanted candor. CEOs who could master straight talk and demonstrate a thorough knowledge of their businesses would be better at executing strategies and increasing stock values. This would build investor trust. As a former investment banker, I knew this approach involved considerably less risk and expense than strategies such as buying and selling companies.

Believing that self-knowledge is essential to making sound wealth-creating decisions, I wanted my CEO clients to see themselves as others saw them. I started to compare their shareholder letters—those most personal of all CEO communications—to the letters signed by their competitors. By contrasting the content in these communications, I could show them which CEOs were the most insightful, engaging, and straightforward.

As I read and analyzed hundreds of shareholder letters, patterns began to emerge. Certain topics appeared in all letters, and other topics—especially ones important to corporate success—rarely appeared. Some CEOs wrote left-brain letters that were analytic, logical, and rational. Other

CEOs wrote right-brain letters that were imaginative, creative, and inspiring. A few CEOs blended the two styles. Some CEOs referred to past promises and events, while other CEOs reported each year as if nothing had happened in previous years. Some wrote clearly; others authored muddled, unintelligible prose.

I sorted these essential topics into a model and assigned each topic a numeric point value. This allowed me to quantify the total content in a letter. For instance, all references to cash and cash flow were coded and scored three points each. Statements of numeric goals scored ten points. Additional points were awarded for corporate stories, emotional words, descriptions of competitive advantages, and other topics, thus increasing the overall score.

Negative points were awarded for spin and confusion. High negative scores revealed CEOs who underestimated investor intelligence and common sense. By adding and subtracting all these positive and negative points, I determined an overall measure of CEO candor. I ranked all the letters from high to low. Then I compared these rankings to the companies' stock price performance and found that the top-scoring companies, on average, consistently outperformed bottom-scoring ones. The numbers confirmed what my mom always told me: It pays to tell the truth.

Trust Corporate Accounting: Know the Culture

Just about everyone believes that numbers can be trusted more than words. And, yes, it is true that numbers *are* more precise than words ("2" is "2," but "to" may also be "too" or even "two"). Nevertheless, it is still critical to know the source of each accounting number.

Columns of figures in a financial statement give the appearance of reliability, but they are merely estimates of value at a given point in time. Once an accounting number is recorded on paper or on a screen, something happens to make this number obsolete. A sale is completed, a loss is recognized, or some other change alters what has been reported.

Never forget that accounting involves human judgments of how to interpret accounting rules. These judgments, in turn, are influenced by the prevailing norms and values of the corporate culture. And a CEO's words can tip us off to these underlying cultural values.

Honest, balanced, and clear CEO shareholder letters give me confidence that I can rely on the company's reported financial numbers. In contrast, I mistrust CEO communications that are evasive and obfuscating. Just review the past letters from Enron or AIG, and you'll see what they reveal. Like lightning bolts in a summer sky, these confusing shareholder letters alert us to approaching storms. They compel us to carefully scrutinize the financial accounting numbers of CEOs who can't or won't communicate clearly.

What Makes Berkshire Hathaway's Letters Different?

We also believe candor benefits us as managers: The CEO who misleads others in public may eventually mislead himself in private.

—BERKSHIRE HATHAWAY OWNER'S MANUAL, PRINCIPLE 12

Just as meteorologists look at atmospheric changes to predict the weather, we can look at shareholder letters to detect shifts in CEO candor. My research shows that this is what Buffett does when he considers an investment in a company. He determines if the CEO writes meaningfully to investors and edits his own copy. He invests in companies with CEOs whose actions show that they believe they are *entrusted* with investor dollars—not *entitled* to them. Consider whether the CEOs of companies you invest with do what Buffett does.

1. Buffett Writes His Own Shareholder Letter

Buffett admits that writing his letter is extremely hard work. It is also vitally strategic. Once he told me, "If you can't write something clearly, it's because you haven't thought it through carefully enough." Importantly, he fears that CEOs who choose to mislead investors in their public letters may eventually mislead themselves in private.

This process of "thinking it through carefully" is essential to Berkshire's risk management strategy. In 2002, I asked Buffett how he could tell if a CEO actually wrote the shareholder letter. He replied, "It's like the Supreme Court's definition of pornography. You just know."

Buffett's assistant, Debbie Bosanek, can vouch for the fact that he writes his own letters. Each year she tries to keep track of the number of drafts he writes. To date, she has failed. Like trying to count snowflakes in a Nebraska blizzard, she gets lost in the changes that fly between her computer and her boss's desk.

Once the past year's letter is completed, Buffett starts anew by jotting down ideas as they come to him. In August, he begins to connect these thoughts on paper. In November, he sends a draft to his friend Carol Loomis, senior editor-at-large at *Fortune*. (Even great CEOs need an outside editor.) When Loomis returns the edited draft, Buffett insists he practically has to start all over again. Finally, the letter is finished in February, just in time to meet annual meeting reporting requirements.

2. Buffett Writes the Longest Shareholder Letter in Corporate America

Buffett's letters average around 12,000 words, roughly six times more words than the average shareholder letter included in my annual CEO Candor™ surveys.

People call his letter the "longest, fastest read" in business. Remember what actress Mae West, the sex goddess of the 1930s, once observed, "It's not the men in my life that count, it's the life in my men." Paraphrasing Ms. West,

Buffett might counter, "It's not the number of words in my letter, it's the life in my words." When asked about the optimal length of a shareholder letter, Buffett said in 2001, "If someone has five or ten thousand dollars invested with you, they ought to be interested enough to read a reasonable amount, so long as you're making it interesting to them."

3. Buffett Imagines He Is Writing to Individual Shareholders and Invites Them to the Berkshire Hathaway Shareholder Weekend

When Buffett writes his shareholder letters, he imagines he's writing them to his sisters, Bertie and Doris, who expect honest, accurate information. Most of their net worth is tied up in Berkshire stock. They want straight answers to predictable questions: Has holding Berkshire stock for the year made them wealthier? What lies ahead for Berkshire? Has Buffett offered plausible future insights? If the sisters detect evasions, family dinners could get uncomfortable. They will demand answers. As Buffett progresses in his letter writing, he replaces his working salutation, "Dear

Bertie and Doris" with "To the shareholders of Berkshire Hathaway."

Buffett invites investors to the Berkshire Hathaway shareholder weekend at the end of his letter. Berkshire's early annual shareholder meetings were held at Omaha's old vaudeville theater. Now shareholders meet in the 1.1 million-square-foot Qwest Center with a 194,000-square-foot exhibition hall and an 18,300-seat arena. Buffett knows how to put on a good show. In 2009, Buffett, age 79, along with straight man Charlie Munger, age 85, started the annual meeting with this introduction: "I'm Warren Buffett, and I have trouble hearing. This is Charlie Munger, and he has trouble seeing. Together, we should be able to answer your questions." Here's the invitation to the meeting from the 2008 shareholder letter:

Our meeting this year will be held on Saturday, May 2nd. As always, the doors will open at the Qwest Center at 7 a.m., and a new Berkshire movie will be shown at 8:30. At 9:30 we will go directly to the question-and-answer period, which (with a break for lunch at the Qwest's stands) will last until 3:00. Then, after a short recess, Charlie and I will convene the annual meeting at 3:15. If you decide to leave during the day's question periods, please do so while Charlie is talking.

The best reason to exit, of course, is to shop. We will help you do that by filling the 194,300-square-foot hall that adjoins the meeting area with the products of Berkshire subsidiaries. Last year, the 31,000 people who came to the meeting did their part, and almost every location racked up record sales. But you can do better. (A friendly warning: If I find sales are lagging, I lock the exits.)

━━

And investors shop—motivated by the shareholder discounts offered by Buffett-owned businesses. In 2008, the Omaha-based Nebraska Furniture Mart racked up $33.3 million in sales in the six-day period before and just after the annual meeting. Buffett hosts a shareholder-only cocktail reception on Friday night at Berkshire's Borsheim's jewelry store and a Sunday afternoon gala where a magician takes coins out of ears; a chess champ takes on all comers—blindfolded; and two world-class bridge experts partner with investors. American Express assigns an agent dedicated just to handle shareholder travel reservations.

4. Buffett Offers Economic Parables

Buffett maintains that Berkshire's investors, like his sisters, may not have MBAs, but they are smart. They want to know what's going on without hearing a lot of jargon and without having the information dumbed down. Even graduates of top business schools can benefit from this approach. Buffett simplifies complexity in his letters by creating economic parables that entertain and also remind readers of fundamental truths.

One of his best parables was written in the aftermath of the bursting of the dot-com bubble. Remember in the late 1990s when technology stocks were hotter than the hinges on the doors to hell? Back then, investor appetite for new issues of dot-com companies was insatiable. People clamored to buy stock in new ventures that lacked revenues, earnings, and cash flow. How did investors justify these purchases? Incredibly, they assumed that the more money a dot-com company spent, the more money it would make. Foolishly, they priced new stock using a multiple of a company's advertising expenses.

Buffett knew that this party would end badly. "We don't understand technology," Buffett reminded investors at his 1999 shareholder meeting, "and we won't invest in it." Those were brave words, but to some they sounded foolhardy. At year-end 1999, Berkshire's performance was at an all-time low. The company's growth in book value was down by 20.5 percent compared to the S&P 500. Pundits declared that Omaha's Oracle had lost his Midas touch.

As fate would have it, in early March 2000, about the same time that Buffett mailed his 1999 shareholder letter, the S&P hit its all-time bubble high mark. By year-end 2000, the S&P had dropped by more than 200 points and Berkshire was up by 59 percent over the S&P 500 benchmark. Buffett did not gloat and say, "I told you so." Ever the teacher, he offered a Cinderella parable in his 2000 shareholder letter to warn investors about the "sedation of effortless money":

The line separating investment and speculation, which is never bright and clear, becomes blurred still further when most market participants have recently enjoyed triumphs. Nothing sedates rationality like large doses of effortless money. After a heady experience of that kind, normally sensible people drift into behavior akin to that of Cinderella at the ball. They know that overstaying the festivities—that is, continuing to speculate in companies that have gigantic valuations relative to the cash they are likely to generate in the future—will eventually bring on pumpkins and mice. But they nevertheless hate to miss a single minute of what is one helluva party. Therefore, the giddy participants all plan to leave just seconds before midnight. There's a problem, though: They are dancing in a room in which the clocks have no hands.

Buffett reminds readers that if something seems too good to be true, most likely it is. The mantra of intelligent investors is always, "Investor beware." Why? To create long-lasting wealth, you must follow Buffett's number one investing rule, "Don't lose money." It is equally important to follow his number two rule: "Don't forget rule number one."

5. Buffett's Blunders: Past, Present, and Future

Berkshire investors gain confidence because Buffett doesn't gloss over his mistakes. He described his biggest all-time blunder in his 2007 letter in a reference to a Bobby Bare country western lyric about going to bed with good-looking women and waking up to find they are ugly. Recalling how in 1993 he paid $433 million for the Dexter Shoe Company, Buffett explained that the company's competitive advantage disappeared within a few years. "To date," he wrote, "Dexter is the worst deal that I've made. But I'll make more mistakes in the future—you can bet on that."

Buffett not only confesses his errors but makes fun of himself. In the same 2007 letter, he reminded investors that he blew an opportunity in 1972 to buy the Dallas–Fort Worth NBC station for $35 million. Back then, his fellow board member Tom Murphy, who was running Capital Cities Broadcasting, needed to divest the station to comply with regulatory requirements. Buffett knew that television stations, which required virtually no capital investment, had excellent growth prospects. They were also likely to "shower cash on their owners." He realized that few other people in the world knew as much about the value of television properties as did Murphy. Yet he said no.

Buffett reported that in the 34 years since turning down the purchase, the station's earnings had totaled at least $1 billion and that its capital value had risen to about $800 million. So what made him reject Murphy's offer? Buffett wrote:

The only explanation is that my brain had gone on vacation and forgotten to notify me. (My behavior resembled that of a politician Molly Ivins once described: "If his I.Q. was any lower, you would have to water him twice a day.")

—

Do shareholders feel better because of his confession? I do. By retelling this story, Buffett is less likely to send his brain on vacation in the future. These public postmortems may not reduce the number of his mistakes—he *is* human— but he is less likely to repeat them. Ego management is a critical and rare CEO skill. Buffett hasn't forgotten what the ancient Greeks taught us about hubris. Believing we are masters of the universe will lead to disaster. By making fun of himself, Buffett keeps it real.

Buffett's decisions to write to shareholders and invite them to the annual meeting, to offer economic parables, and to keep his ego in check are ones seldom repeated by other CEOs. Since 2000, Buffett has offered shareholders one other innovation. He begins his letter with a long table of numbers. It shows the year-over-year growth in wealth from 1965 to the present time. This is Buffett's report card to his investors.

What Is the Berkshire Hathaway Report Card?

Our long-term economic goal is to maximize Berkshire's average annual rate of gain in intrinsic business value on a per-share basis.

—BERKSHIRE HATHAWAY OWNER'S MANUAL, PRINCIPLE 3

Most CEOs measure their corporate success by tracking the minute-to-minute changes in their company stock prices. Not Buffett. He refuses to be distracted by Berkshire's short-term market movements. He focuses instead on a *long-term economic goal*, to grow *per share intrinsic business value*. This mission is the key to understanding Buffett's Midas touch.

Berkshire's Long-Term Economic Goal

Buffett is a balance sheet guy. That's where the cash is reported. The amount of cash in a business is found at the top of the list of corporate assets. Cash is the fuel that drives economic value. In a financial crisis, when banks cannot lend, cash is particularly valuable.

Most CEOs, however, focus on growth in corporate profits more than on cash and balance sheet growth. They record profits in the company's income statements by reporting total revenues and deducting expenses. This is the corporate "bottom line." While these profits (a.k.a. earnings) may look reliable, investors who focus on long-term wealth know better. The source of the problem is simple: Some of the reported expenses in these income statements are cash, and some are determined by accounting rules. As a result, earnings include both cash and noncash (i.e., "accounting") numbers. Buffett cares most about the cash part.

Cash is real. It means that the company has immediate funds to pay vendors' bills, employee wages, and interest expenses. Noncash earnings include credits for cash that was used to make past purchases, such as buying large equipment that depreciates over time. Noncash earnings can also be credits for money owed in the future, such as deferred taxes. Noncash earnings are subject to accounting interpretations. They can be adjusted to inflate earnings and boost the stock price. But it is harder to fiddle with the cash numbers.

Buffett won't let noncash earnings influence his investment choices. His long-term cash obsession creates unique opportunities that others miss.

Remember when the stock market dropped to new lows in 2008, a casualty of the global financial crisis? Cash dried up. Banks were unable or unwilling to lend. People panicked. Not Buffett. He compares the stock market to a butcher's shop. Do we panic when the price of filet mignon drops? No, we rejoice. Who wouldn't want to buy the highest-quality steaks at chopped meat prices? Buffett keeps a lot of cash on hand in order to be ready for unique crisis-born opportunities.

At the end of June 2008, cash represented just over 11 percent of Buffett's balance sheet. He used some of it to provide high-cost financing for then top-credit-rated companies Goldman Sachs and GE, both desperately in need of cash. He announced his biggest acquisition to date—

buying the Burlington Northern Santa Fe Railway for $34 billion. At $100 a share, he paid a reasonable, but not a cheap, price. Pundits scratched their heads trying to find the sizzle in his announcement. Most were stumped. They don't understand intrinsic value.

The Secret to Building Wealth: Grow Intrinsic Value

Intrinsic value is an estimate of the future cash and earning power of a business over its expected lifetime. Buffett admits that calculating intrinsic value is difficult; it is an art as much as a science. It requires mathematical discipline and experience to ascribe value to corporate reputation, management quality, and other intangible factors of business success. Here is the simplified version of the steps Buffett follows:

1. Evaluate tangible and intangible assets in order to estimate the annual amount of cash flows a business or investment will generate over its expected lifetime.

2. Factor in a rate for the impact of future inflation, and discount or reduce the value of the business cash flows by this assumed rate.

3. Deduct extra points for the kind of business risk you expect. (Buffett adds this step to build in a margin of safety in the event that his assumptions don't pan out.)

4. Divide this sum by the number of shares outstanding in the business.

Voilà! You've arrived at *per-share intrinsic value.*

Now compare this number to the discounted cash flows when buying virtually risk-free Treasury bonds. If the intrinsic value of the business investment is higher, it passes Buffett's economic test. It is an investment worthy of consideration for your portfolio.

Since few of us possess Buffett's business acumen, he gives us a proxy for Berkshire's intrinsic value: per-share book value. Book value is measured in dollars by the sum of all business assets—what a business has—minus its liabilities—what it owes. When this number is positive and shows growth, you have the makings of a healthy business. If it is negative, you need to look more closely.

Buffett wants Berkshire's stock to trade at a fair, not an inflated, value, as close as possible to intrinsic value or book value. In his shareholder letters, he strives to communicate in ways that support this goal.

Per-Share Discipline: Don't Dilute

Per-share discipline is essential to understanding how Buffett evaluates companies. He doesn't stop at comparing the growth in total year-over-year earnings. He needs to know how a company grows earnings per share (EPS). This EPS metric is vital; it measures how much of a company each shareholder owns. Here's a simple example:

Imagine that Great Intrinsic Value Enterprise Inc. (GIVE) has 1 million shares outstanding and earned $5 million in the past year. To calculate the company's earnings per share, you simply divide the dollars earned by the number of shares outstanding. Now you can see that GIVE's EPS is $5.00 per share. In other words, each share of stock you own entitles you to $5.00 of earnings. Assume that you personally own 100,000 shares of the company or 10 percent of all the stock. You would be entitled to $500,000 of earnings in that year.

Imagine that the CEO of GIVE decided to sell 4 million additional shares in the company at $10 a pop to buy manufacturing equipment and increase its output of mobile homes. Now a total of 5 million GIVE shares are outstanding. Assuming no other changes, the EPS of the company has dropped to $1.00. Your 100,000 shares now translate to only $100,000 of earnings. Your ownership has been diluted. This is why Buffett focuses on per-share results. He tries to avoid issuing new stock. He doesn't want to dilute investor interests.

Of course, the picture brightens if the company is able to increase earnings by making great mobile homes. Assume that in two years, the company has sold enough new homes to double GIVE's total earnings to $10 million. No new shares have been issued, so the total shares outstanding are still 5 million. You can see that GIVE's EPS two years later is now $2.00 a share, or $10 million divided by 5 million shares.

Can you see the problem? GIVE's earnings and EPS have doubled. You continue to own 100,000 shares, but now your investment buys less of the earnings (and the company) than it did before the stock sale. This is why Buffett hates to issue stock to buy companies and pay for capital expenditures. He prefers to grow Berkshire by investing internally generated cash.

Back to Dexter Shoe: Giving Away More in Value than You Receive

In 1993, Buffett bought Dexter Shoe for $433 million. To pay for this purchase, he used 25,203 shares of Berkshire's "A" stock. These shares represented 1.6 percent of the company's total shares.

By 2007, Berkshire had grown, and its stock had appreciated. The company was now valued at about $220 billion, up from roughly $19 billion. The 1.6 percent interest in the company that Buffett had given up to buy Dexter had skyrocketed to about $3.5 billion. By using stock instead of cash, his error in buying Dexter was magnified. "In essence," he explained, "I gave away 1.6 percent of a wonderful business—one now valued at $220 billion—to buy a worthless business."

Remember this per-share math the next time you hear a company talk about making a large acquisition with company stock. Are the company executives explaining how much more the new acquisition must generate in per-share profits in order to compensate investors for the per-share dilution in their equity? If so, your managers may be disciplined cash allocators. To be certain, look at their track record.

Buffett warns investors that as Berkshire grows bigger, it will be more difficult to show per-share growth. It's the law of large numbers. To move the growth needle, Berkshire will need to find elephant-sized investments. Buffett admits that these are harder to find. In addition, once located, they often command pachyderm-sized prices. By measuring the per-share contributions of these larger acquisitions, Buffett will judge whether they can add meaningfully to Berkshire's future economic growth.

Berkshire Report Card: Relative Results

Now you know the three building blocks that make up Berkshire's report card: (1) pursuit of an economic/cash goal, (2) focus on intrinsic/book value, and (3) maintaining per-share discipline. Take a look at the table on pages 43–44 from Buffett's 2008 letter to shareholders.

The first column is the reporting year. The second column shows the annual percentage change in the per-share book value of Berkshire. The third column shows the annual percentage change in the Standard & Poor's 500 stock index, including dividends, which measures market performance. We know that Buffett's goal is to see that Berkshire's book/intrinsic value beats the market. The fourth column nets these two numbers to show if he has succeeded.

As you look down the fourth column, you will note that the year-over-year growth in Berkshire's per-share book value exceeded the growth in the S&P 500 stock price index in all but six years (1967, 1975, 1980, 1999, 2003, and 2004). This is an impressive feat. No other company can show this kind of performance.

Now look at the bottom line. How have Berkshire's earliest investors benefited from Buffett's pursuit of a *long-term economic goal*? From 1965 to 2008, Berkshire's annual compounded gain in per-share book value was 20.3 percent, 11.4 percent better than the S&P 500. Compare the

Berkshire's Corporate Performance vs. the S&P 500		
	ANNUAL PERCENTAGE CHANGE	
Year	in Per-Share Book Value of Berkshire (1)	in S&P 500 with Dividends Included (2)	Relative Results (1) – (2)
1965	23.8	10.0	13.8
1966	20.3	(11.7)	32.0
1967	11.0	30.9	(19.9)
1968	19.0	11.0	8.0
1969	16.2	(8.4)	24.6
1970	12.0	3.9	8.1
1971	16.4	14.6	1.8
1972	21.7	18.9	2.8
1973	4.7	(14.8)	19.5
1974	5.5	(26.4)	31.9
1975	21.9	37.2	(15.3)
1976	59.3	23.6	35.7
1977	31.9	(7.4)	39.3
1978	24.0	6.4	17.6
1979	35.7	18.2	17.5
1980	19.3	32.3	(13.0)
1981	31.4	(5.0)	36.4
1982	40.0	21.4	18.6
1983	32.3	22.4	9.9
1984	13.6	6.1	7.5
1985	48.2	31.6	16.6
1986	26.1	18.6	7.5
1987	19.5	5.1	14.4
1988	20.1	16.6	3.5

	ANNUAL PERCENTAGE CHANGE		
Year	in Per-Share Book Value of Berkshire (1)	in S&P 500 with Dividends Included (2)	Relative Results (1) – (2)
1989	44.4	31.7	12.7
1990	7.4	(3.1)	10.5
1991	39.6	30.5	9.1
1992	20.3	7.6	12.7
1993	14.3	10.1	4.2
1994	13.9	1.3	12.6
1995	43.1	37.6	5.5
1996	31.8	23.0	8.8
1997	34.1	33.4	.7
1998	48.3	28.6	19.7
1999	.5	21.0	(20.5)
2000	6.5	(9.1)	15.6
2001	(6.2)	(11.9)	5.7
2002	10.0	(22.1)	32.1
2003	21.0	28.7	(7.7)
2004	10.5	10.9	(.4)
2005	6.4	4.9	1.5
2006	18.4	15.8	2.6
2007	11.0	5.5	5.5
2008	(9.6)	(37.0)	27.4
Compounded Annual Gain: 1965–2008	20.3%	8.9%	11.4
Overall Gain— 1964–2008	362,319%	4,276%	

value in 1965 with Berkshire's compounded gain by 2008. Berkshire is up by 362,319 percent versus a mere 4,276 percent increase for the S&P 500.

This performance supports Buffett's decision not to pay out dividends in 45 years in business. He has been able to reinvest Berkshire's profits at rates considerably higher than Berkshire's investors could have earned by reinvesting them in the market. When the company can no longer meet the test of reinvesting $1.00 of EPS to create $1.00 of additional value, then, says Buffett, Berkshire will pay dividends and let his owner-partners reinvest the cash.

Buffett's six-digit results underscore the value of pursuing a per-share economic discipline. As will be shown in Chapter 5, this same focus allows him to find low-cost capital to produce these numbers. To understand Buffett's wealth-creating genius, it's necessary to see where Buffett finds low-cost capital to invest and how he allocates it.

Is Warren Buffett a CEO or a CCAO?

Let's look at the prototype of a dream business, our own See's Candy.

—BERKSHIRE HATHAWAY 2007 SHAREHOLDER LETTER

Business schools teach that the job of a CEO is to set and execute strategy. At Berkshire Hathaway, the CEO is first and foremost the CCAO (Chief Capital Allocation Officer). Buffett executes strategy based on his capital allocation principles. These principles are his navigation system. After four decades dedicated to charting a course at the helm of Berkshire, Buffett has added considerably more cash-producing cargo to this business.

The Hunt for Low-Cost Capital

The secret of Buffett's success lies in finding low-cost capital to invest. This is why he is drawn to the insurance business. In 2008, 24 percent of Berkshire's revenues and over 50 percent of its profits were generated by the company's property-casualty, auto insurance (GEICO), sophisticated reinsurance, and other insurance businesses.

Like bees to honey, Buffett is attracted to the "float" that insurance businesses generate. Float is created when Berkshire receives insurance premium but does not have to pay claims until some future time. When the premium dollars exceed claims and underwriting expenses, Berkshire generates an underwriting profit. By consistently posting profits, Buffett essentially gets "free money" to invest. When Berkshire's investments generate positive returns, it is like getting paid to hold free money.

Buffett counts deferred taxes as another debtlike source of low-cost capital funds. Because these tax liabilities are paid in the future, cash is freed up for investments. It is like a government loan. As long as the company grows, this virtual loan continues to increase. If growth stops, then this account begins to decline.

At the end of 2008, Berkshire's net deferred tax liabilities totaled $8 billion and its float was $58 billion. Investing this low-cost capital at higher returns becomes harder as Berkshire grows. It is the law of large numbers. Ever bigger acquisitions are needed to move the growth needle.

Buffett charts Berkshire's progress by tracking relative, not absolute, results. He wants to post better-than-market results and show that capital works harder at Berkshire than at other companies. To understand how Buffett has grown Berkshire's low-cost capital and produced a 45-year record of unbeatable growth, a little history is in order. This history will also explain why Wall Street was slow to recognize the value of Buffett's business masterpiece.

From the Canyons of Wall Street to the Plains of Omaha

From 1954 to 1956, Buffett dissected balance sheets as a Wall Street stock analyst at the Graham-Newman investment company. When the founders closed the business to pursue other interests, Buffett hotfooted it back to Omaha. On May 1, 1956, he founded Buffett Associates, Ltd. with early partners who included his sister Doris and her husband, his Aunt Alice, his father-in-law, his lawyer, Dan Monen, a former college roommate, and the roommate's mother. They raised $105,000. To keep overhead low, he operated the partnership out of his rented home. He was 25 years old.

Early on, Buffett spelled out what his partners could expect. He would take money only from those who agreed to play by his rules. First, he would not tell partners where their money was invested. He needed their trust. Second, the fund's results would be reported only once a year. Third, Buffett would not reduce partner returns by taking fees and overrides. In fact, he would get paid only if the fund made a profit. If the fund performed poorly, he got zilch. At year end, he wrote long letters to his partners explaining how they were wealthier. Each year he warned that it would be impossible to beat the prior year's results, but he did just that. By February 1959, he was managing more than $1.0 million in seven different investment partnerships. In 1962, he consolidated these into one entity, Buffett Partnership, Ltd. The assets now totaled $7.2 million.

Buffett devoured annual reports, looking for value that wasn't reflected in stock prices. In late 1962, he began buying shares of Massachusetts-based textile manufacturer Berkshire Hathaway. At $7.60, the shares traded at a significant discount to the company's net working capital of $16.50. What created this gap? The company's proud management had invested new capital to improve the company's mills. But fierce competition had forced down textile prices. Investors questioned whether management could recover this capital and earn a return on it.

Berkshire's stock continued to trade below book value, and Buffett continued to buy. By 1965, he owned enough shares to take control of the company. The average per-share cost of the shares he had bought was $14.86, still below the per share net working capital of $19.00. He got the plants and equipment for free. But could Berkshire be made profitable? Buffett was named a company director and installed career employee Ken Chace as CEO. Chace ran the mills, and Buffett managed the money. Giving Chace just enough cash to keep the business going, Buffett chose to use the rest to make investments outside the textile industry.

In 1967, he bought National Indemnity Insurance Company for $8.6 million. In 1968, he bought shares in Blue Chip Stamps. Like today's airline mileage programs, the company earned fees from grocery stores that gave Blue Chip stamps to shoppers for grocery purchases. Over time, shoppers traded in their stamps for appliances and other rewards. The attraction for Buffett was the substantial float in cash that resulted between receiving grocers' income and redeeming stamps. In 1969, Buffett bought the Illinois National Bank & Trust of Rockford. Both Gene Abegg, the CEO of the Illinois National Bank & Trust, and Jack Ringwalt of National Indemnity shared important Buffett traits: They were tight with shareholder money, honest, and devoted to their work. Both started their businesses from scratch.

By 1969, the stock market had reached new highs, and the Buffett Partnership continued to beat its returns. As the market continued to climb even higher, Buffett announced that he would close his partnerships. The partners were stunned. Early investors had seen an initial investment of $10,000 grow to $260,000. Over 13 years, they had realized an annual compound rate of 31.6 percent, substantially greater than the 9.1 percent gain in the Dow Jones Industrial Average. Still, Buffett wanted out. He told the partners that the speculation-driven stock market didn't make sense; he wanted no part of the folly. He had been working nonstop and wanted to broaden his interests.

Buffett sold everything in the portfolio except for shares in Diversified Retailing, Blue Chip Stamps, and

Berkshire Hathaway, which now included insurance and banking businesses as well as equity investments. As Buffett liquidated his funds, the partners were offered a choice: take their distributions in cash or in pro-rata stock of each of the three surviving companies, alongside Buffett. Avoiding the speculative market, Buffett continued to hunt for attractive underated businesses. In 1971, he bought a controlling interest in See's Candies.

By early January 1973, the Dow had climbed to an all-time high of 1,051 points. But only $17 million of Berkshire's $101 million insurance portfolio was invested in stocks; the rest was in bonds. Not long after this high, the market swooned. Then it ratcheted down further. By October 1974, it hit a low of 580 points. Investors panicked, but Buffett rejoiced. He was in his element once again. Over the following years, Buffett bagged big game at bargain prices, adding Wesco Financial, a Pasadena-based savings and loan, and buying large blocks of stock in *The Washington Post* and GEICO. In 1977, Buffett bought *The Buffalo News*. His annual shareholder letters were circulating more widely among investors who shared Buffett's belief that analyzing the substance and character of a business was the holy grail of investing. Guessing a price that someone else was willing to pay—irrespective of fundamentals—was not.

Wall Street Is Late to the Party

In 1999, after 34 years in business, Berkshire had a market capitalization that positioned it as the 74th largest American company. Yet it had no Wall Street research coverage. Stock analysts largely ignored Buffett's masterpiece. Was it an investment company or a bona fide operating company? Was Buffett a CEO or an investment manager? Wall Street could not figure out Buffett's unconventional methods, nor did it pay for them to do the research on Berkshire. Since banks paid for stock research from trading profits, Berkshire was a dud. Only meager profits could be gained from trading Berkshire stock. Its loyal investors didn't want to let it go.

All this changed in 1999 when Alice Schroeder, a Paine Webber research analyst, wrote the first Wall Street research report on Berkshire. She concluded that Berkshire was a conglomerate—a mix of different operating businesses with a sizable investment portfolio. But unlike other conglomerates, the businesses that Berkshire owned did not enjoy synergies. Each company operated independently and sent the capital it did not need to Buffett to invest for Berkshire's owners.

Berkshire in 2010 is a great deal bigger, but its playbook has not changed much. Buffett continues to rely on his managers to run their day-to-day business operations. He continues to devote precious time to reading and thinking. Like a miner panning for gold, he sifts data from newspapers, annual reports, and other publications, looking for gaps in values that others miss.

The Berkshire Capital Allocation Checklist

To determine the attractiveness of businesses as investments, Buffett uses a simple checklist. To meet his tests, companies must possess (1) "a sensible price tag" (be economically sound); (2) "durable competitive advantages" (enjoy a wide moat); and (3) businesses that he can understand (be within his "circle of competence"). Finally, Buffett will invest only in companies with managers who are passionately involved in their business creations. These leaders don't need money. They work because they love what they do.

Even though he is not involved in the day-to-day operations, Buffett pays close attention to how much cash each business generates. He determines how much is needed to maintain a rate of appropriate growth and how much can be invested elsewhere to build intrinsic value in the Berkshire enterprise.

In his 2007 shareholder letter, Buffett offered a capsule view of how he assesses companies based on their capital allocation profiles. He sorts businesses into three categories based on the cost of business growth: great, good, and gruesome. This sorting allows him to see sizzle where others cannot.

See's Candies: A Great, Not Just a Good, Business

Buffett puts See's Candies into the "great" category. Most CEOs would not. In 2007, Sees sold 31 pounds of chocolate, a growth rate of only 2 percent. What does Buffett see that others miss? First, See's meets Buffett's economic criteria: He paid a sensible price for the business. Second, the company enjoys a durable competitive advantage: Its quality chocolate is bought by legions of loyal customers. Third, it is a business he understands. And fourth, it has great managers. But the company possesses one more attraction that gives it star quality: It throws off cash and requires very little capital to grow. Buffett explains See's value proposition in his 2007 shareholder letter:

We bought See's [in 1972] for $25 million when its sales were $30 million and pre-tax earnings were less than $5 million. The capital then required to conduct the business was $8 million. (Modest seasonal debt was also needed for a few months each year.) Consequently, the company was earning 60% pre-tax on invested capital. Two factors helped to minimize the funds required for operations. First, the product was sold for cash, and that eliminated accounts receivable. Second, the production and distribution cycle was short, which minimized inventories.

Last year See's sales were $383 million, and pre-tax profits were $82 million. The capital now required to run the business is $40 million. This means we have had to reinvest only $32 million since 1972 to handle the modest physical growth—and somewhat immodest financial growth—of the business. In the meantime pre-tax earnings have totaled $1.35 billion. All of that, except for the $32 million, has been sent to Berkshire.

Buffett uses See's cash to buy other attractive businesses. Getting biblical, he noted:

Just as Adam and Eve kick-started an activity that led to six billion humans, See's has given birth to multiple new streams of cash for us. (The biblical command to "be fruitful and multiply" is one we take seriously at Berkshire.) . . . There's no rule that you have to invest money where you've earned it. Indeed, it's often a mistake to do so: Truly great businesses, earning huge returns on tangible assets, can't for any extended period reinvest a large portion of their earnings internally at high rates of return.

But a company like slow-growing See's is rare in corporate America. In order to grow earnings like See's, CEOs in other businesses typically would need "to invest $400 million, not the $32 million" that See's required. Why is this true? Because most growing businesses "have both working capital needs that increase in proportion to sales growth and significant requirements for fixed asset investments." Not so at See's.

FlightSafety: A Good, Not a Great, Business

Berkshire's FlightSafety business, acquired in 1996, is the poster child for a "good" business. Like See's, it possesses a durable competitive advantage as the leading provider of airline pilot training. Going to a different company, says Buffett, would be "like taking the low bid on a surgical procedure"—a frightening image when you are strapped into a narrow seat 35,000 feet above the earth. How does FlightSafety rank on the amount of capital it needs to grow? Not great, but good.

Each year, the company must invest in new flight simulators to train pilots to fly new planes. Each simulator costs roughly $12 million; they aren't cheap. Buffett counts FlightSafety as a good business, "but far from a See's-like return—return on an incremental investment of $509 million." He explains:

[I]f measured only by economic returns, Flight-Safety is an excellent but not extraordinary business. Its put-up-more-to-earn-more experience is that faced by most corporations. For example, our large investment in regulated utilities falls squarely in this category. We will earn considerably more money in this business ten years from now, but we will invest many billions to make it.

Buffett never forgets that growth is good, but only at a reasonable cost.

Gruesome Businesses: Think Airlines

A gruesome business is one that grows rapidly, requires a lot of capital, and earns meager profits. The poster child for a gruesome business is any airline where competitive advantages are hard to find. Buffett explains:

[A] durable competitive advantage [in the airline industry] has proven elusive ever since the days of the Wright Brothers. Indeed, if a farsighted capitalist had been present at Kitty Hawk, he would have done his successors a huge favor by shooting Orville down.

The airline industry's demand for capital ever since that first flight has been insatiable. Investors have poured money into a bottomless pit, attracted by growth when they should have been repelled by it. And I, to my shame, participated in this foolishness when I had Berkshire buy U.S. Air preferred stock in 1989. As the ink was drying on our check, the company went into a tailspin, and before long our preferred dividend was no longer being paid. But we then got very lucky. In one of the recurrent, but always misguided, bursts of optimism for airlines, we were actually able to sell our shares in 1998 for a hefty gain. In the decade following our sale, the company went bankrupt. Twice.

Capital Allocation and Savings Accounts

Buffett compares these three different types of great, good, and gruesome businesses to "savings accounts." The great business is like an account that "pays an extraordinarily high interest rate that will rise as the years pass. A good one pays an attractive rate of interest that will be earned also on deposits that are added. Finally, the gruesome account both pays an inadequate interest rate and requires you to keep adding money at those disappointing returns."

Now it is easy to see why Buffett's attraction to See's is not just the candy. The company is a chocolate-powered cash machine. Buffett's ability to allocate capital wisely and grow long-term economic value at Berkshire has produced his unbeatable track record. But he has not done this alone. He enjoys investor support. In fact, he has attracted what are arguably the most loyal investors on the planet. Their loyalty allows him to tap dance to work every day.

Why Does Buffett Tap-Dance to Work Every Day?

> *In line with Berkshire's owner orientation, most of our directors have a major portion of their net worth invested in the company. We eat our own cooking.*
>
> —BERKSHIRE HATHAWAY OWNER'S MANUAL, PRINCIPLE 2

Not many CEOs live within walking distance of their workplace. Even fewer will claim that they love their jobs so much that they tap-dance to work. Buffett does; and why not? He enjoys by far the most loyal shareholders in the world, owner-partners who stick with him in both up and down markets. Before you learn how he builds investor loyalty, you need to know that Berkshire has two classes of stock and that Buffett owns, by far, more of both classes of stock than anyone else.

Country Club Prices

Investors can choose whether they want to become Berkshire Class A or Class B stockholders. Price is a consideration. The Class A stock trades at country-club prices. It is the most expensive stock on the New York Stock Exchange. Between 2004 and 2009, the stock traded as high as $149,000 a share and averaged over $103,000. Since few people can afford to buy even one share, investors tend to hold their stock for a long time. It's not just a purchase; it's a commitment. They watch it grow.

Investors who bought Berkshire in the early days, when it cost only $18, hold onto their shares. Why sell and pay hefty capital gains taxes? As a result, the turnover in Berkshire stock is significantly lower than the average turnover of stocks traded on the Exchange.

In 1996, Wall Street merchandisers tried to create a mutual fund that copied Buffett's stock picks and holdings. This new fund would attract investors who wanted a piece of Berkshire but could not afford the high sticker price. But the venture violated Buffett's fairness principles. First, small investors would end up paying high fees to buy these new mutual fund shares. Second, the Wall Streeters would pocket fat sales commissions simply by riding Buffett's coattails. Applying the "if you can't lick them" strategy, he created a new Class B share that would trade at 1/30th the value of an Class A share. It lowered the price of entry into the kingdom of Berkshire to about $1,200 a share and stopped the merchandisers.

Consider that Class B stockholders get only 1/200 of a vote in company matters. Yet despite having only symbolic voting rights, these investors are about as loyal as the Class A shareholders. Both Classes A and B investors trust Buffett to look out for their interests. As Berkshire's largest shareholder, he reminds them that he eats his own cooking.

Buffett Eats His Own Cooking

At year-end 2009, Buffett owned just over 31 percent of all Berkshire's Class A shares and 9 percent of all Class B shares. Consider that the next eight largest individual owners of Class A stock owned just over 3.2 percent and the total shares owned by the top 100 institutional holders accounted for 23 percent of the Class A shares. The rest of the shares were held primarily by individual shareholders.

Why do investors trust Buffett to look out for their interests? Simple. It's because he eats his own cooking. Buffett not only owns a lot of Berkshire stock, but this stock represents the bulk of his family's net worth. Similarly, Vice Chair Munger's ownership in Berkshire accounts for a sizable share of his family's net worth. Investors can sleep better at night knowing that the two top executives have significant skin in the game. Buffett explains:

Charlie and I cannot promise you results. But we can guarantee that your financial fortunes will move in lockstep with ours for whatever period of time you elect to be our partner. We have no interest in large salaries or options or other means of gaining an "edge" over you. We want to make money only when our partners do and in exactly the same proportion. Moreover, when I do something dumb, I want you to be able to derive some solace from the fact that my financial suffering is proportional to yours.

In other words, when Berkshire's stock drops, Buffett's net worth declines accordingly. Berkshire investors know that Buffett shares their pain and will be motivated to do better in the future. He is out to attract intelligent, long-term investors who appreciate a CEO who gets wealthy in tandem with shareholders and not from executive perks and golden parachutes.

CEO Compensation That Never Changes

Buffett's compensation is different from that of most CEOs of publicly traded companies. Rather than expect his board to approve millions of dollars in compensation, Buffett asks his directors not to increase his salary. This directive was reported in the 2008 Berkshire Hathaway proxy:

Mr. Buffett's compensation is reviewed annually by the Governance, Compensation and Nominating Committee ("Committee") of the Corporation's Board of Directors. Due to Mr. Buffett's desire that his compensation remain unchanged, the Committee has not proposed an increase in Mr. Buffett's compensation since the Committee was created in 2004. Prior to that time Mr. Buffett recommended to the Board of Directors the amount of his compensation. Mr. Buffett's annual compensation has been $100,000 for over the last 25 years and he would not expect or desire it to increase in the future.

At Berkshire, compensation is based on growth in per-share value. The company doesn't offer stock options, which dilute shareholder interests. Since bigger is not always better at Berkshire, don't expect managers to get paid just for adding assets. When Buffett writes that the "size of our paychecks or our offices will never be related to the size of Berkshire's balance sheet" he's not joking. Since 1962, when Berkshire moved into its present offices, the world headquarters has grown from about 500 square feet to 10,686 square feet. At the end of 2009, the Berkshire empire was run by just 21 employees.

Explain Accounting: Teach and Trust

Buffett educates his investors about accounting so that they can understand how the company makes money. He offers miniseminars in his shareholder letters about measures and concepts like insurance float and goodwill. Each explanation helps investors to value Buffett's approach to management and to determine whether he is growing shareholder capital.

Buffett admits that understanding Berkshire's accounting is no walk in the park. He warns his owner-partners that conventional accounting rules will tell them very little about the company's "true economic performance." Instead, he chooses to report on "the earnings of each major business we control. . . . These figures, along with other information we will supply about the individual businesses, should generally aid you in making judgments about them."

Anticipating investor concerns about full, honest disclosure, Buffett reminds investors that he will try to be forthright about both unhappy and happy experiences. He writes in the Owner's Manual at Berkshire, "you will find no 'big bath' accounting maneuvers or restructurings or any 'smoothing' of quarterly or annual results. We will always tell you how many strokes we have taken on each hole and never play around with the scorecard. When the numbers are a very rough 'guesstimate,' as they necessarily must be in insurance reserving, we will try to be both consistent and conservative in our approach."

Treat Investors Fairly: Sell Stock at Full Value

Buffett builds a loyal following by striving to treat all investors fairly. For example, he refuses to meet with individual shareholders during the year—neither Class A nor Class B shareholders. He discloses all company financial information on the Internet at a preannounced time so that no one investor can get a leg up on other investors. He refuses to give earnings guidance.

Buffett wants Berkshire's stock to trade close to its intrinsic value at all times. He wants his investors to receive as much in per-share business value when they sell their Berkshire shares as when they first buy them. Consequently, he will not sell new Berkshire shares at a discount. In 1996, when Berkshire issued the new Class B shares, Buffett shocked the market by declaring that these shares were not undervalued. He asked, "Why would owner-partners want manager-partners to deliberately sell assets for 80 cents that in fact are worth a dollar? We didn't commit that kind of crime in our offering of Class B shares and we never will."

Buffett's commitment to treating investors fairly and maintaining Berkshire's intrinsic value flies in the face of Wall Street practices. Typically, Wall Street underwriters buy new stock issues from their corporate clients and put billions of dollars of their firm's capital at risk. They are betting they can sell the stock—quickly—and pocket sales commissions and price appreciation. Having unsold inventory at the end of the day is a potential disaster. This overhang could cause the price of the new issue to decline, thus angering early buyers and damaging the firm's reputation as a trustworthy underwriter. Discounting the price of the new stock helps them to unload inventory fast and maintain pricing integrity.

Yet this practice violates Buffett's desire to treat all investors fairly. This equity standard, along with Buffett's track record, helps to explain why Berkshire's shareholders are content to hear from him only once a year. It underscores the reason they will pony up from four to six figures for a single share of stock.

As the owner of a business where he eats his own cooking, Buffett tells investors not to expect the standard fare they get from other CEOs. Berkshire *has no* investor relations department. Indeed, Buffett *is* the corporate communications *and* investor relations departments. While shareholders can call the company to get routine information about stock holdings or the annual meeting, they won't get information on why NetJet's sales are down in Europe or what stocks look attractive to Buffett. There are no investor relations professionals to talk to. Instead, callers are directed to the company Web site to read news releases.

Remember that the entirety of Berkshire's investor communications activities includes only the annual shareholder letter, the Berkshire annual meeting, event-driven press releases such as quarterly earnings and announcements of acquisitions or other material changes, and financial reports required by the Securities and Exchange Commission (SEC). Now you can see why Buffett's shareholder letter is so important. Each year he must renew investor trust through this communication.

Skeptics wonder if the investor loyalty that Buffett enjoys has turned him into the Pied Piper of Wall Street. Rather than seeing an investor community united by common principles, they suspect that Berkshire has an unquestioning cult following. My guess is that few of these cynics have ever read his shareholder letters carefully. If they did, they would find that Buffett wants to open, not to close, the minds of his investors.

Read the "bites" in Chapters 7 and 8 for the wisdom that Buffett imparts. These groundbreaking bites from his shareholder letter offer sound views on accounting and economic value. Never before in the history of capitalism has a CEO communicated with his partners by following the golden rule: Give investors the information you would like to have if you were in their place.

II

Bite-Sized
Investor Truths

Buffett's shareholder letters document his journey to understanding that financial markets lack inherent logic in the short term, human emotions handicap rational judgments, and how finding economic value is the key to wealth building. His letters underpin his steadfast commitment to shareowner partnership. Now that you have some grounding in the capital allocation principles that shape Buffett's shareholder letters, use these "bites" like 3-D glasses. They will help you to extract valuable information from his annual reports and apply this learning when reading communications of other CEOs.

When Buffett's letter was released over the Internet on February 28, 2009, the pundits misrepresented his report, quoting only part of the sentence: "the economy will be in shambles . . ." They left out "this does not tell us whether the stock market will rise or fall." Had you ignored the pundits, you might have ventured into the market as it dipped down to its lowest level since 1996. If you had bought and held stocks of companies with durable competitive advantages, sound economics, and good managers—you would be wealthier today.

This guide protects you against shortsighted punditry. The following 25 bites, or investment tips, are inspired by Buffett's 2008 shareholder letter. Each bite features a Buffett quote and is accompanied by commentary that underscores a key principle. Each ends with a moral, a lesson to boost your financial I.Q.

The tips have been divided into two chapters: "How to Spot Great Businesses Run by Great Managers" and "How to Become an Intelligent Investor." After you have digested these bites, we return to one of the most puzzling questions about Warren Buffett: Why, given his unbeatable track record, do CEOs, boards of directors, and influential investors ignore his principles?

How to Spot Great Businesses Run by Great Managers

We have long invested in derivatives contracts that Charlie and I think are mispriced, just as we try to invest in mispriced stocks and bonds.... The dangers that derivatives pose for both participants and society—dangers of which we've long warned, and that can be dynamite—arise when these contracts lead to leverage and/or counterparty risk that is extreme. At Berkshire nothing like that has occurred—nor will it.

—BERKSHIRE HATHAWAY 2009 SHAREHOLDER LETTER

BITE

No. 1

Find CEOs Who Treasure Cash

As the year progressed, a series of life-threatening problems within many of the world's great financial institutions was unveiled. This led to a dysfunctional credit market that in important respects soon turned non-functional. The watchword throughout the country became the creed I saw on restaurant walls when I was young: *"In God we trust; all others pay cash."*

By the fourth quarter, the credit crisis, coupled with tumbling home and stock prices, had produced a paralyzing fear that engulfed the country. A freefall in business activity ensued, accelerating at a pace that I have never before witnessed. The U.S.—and much of the world—became trapped in

a vicious negative-feedback cycle. Fear led to
business contraction, and that in turn led to even
greater fear.

———

Buffett reminds us that cash can be trusted. He runs his insurance company by keeping more money on hand than
just about any other similarly sized or even larger public
corporation. Not only does he need cash to meet the insurance claims of policyholders, but he also wants to invest
cash in new and attractive opportunities. However, as
Berkshire has grown, these opportunities have been more
difficult to find.

The smart money scoffs at keeping large levels of corporate cash. But these people ignore what Buffett never
forgets—a coin has two sides. Just as we are now trapped
in a vicious negative-feedback cycle, only yesterday we were
trapped in a vicious positive-feedback cycle. You remember: Mortgage money flowed like milk and honey, housing
prices climbed ever upward, and people believed that this
trend would continue forever. They literally bet the ranch.

But in financial markets, what is up will come down, and what is down is likely to go up. Buffett wants to be prepared for both eventualities. He repeatedly warned us about the price we would pay for our bubble addictions. Still, no one ever imagined how serious the consequences would be. In the wake of the credit collapse of 2008, fear and loathing have spread like wildfire. Can we use this crisis to re-create a vibrant global economy so that our children and grandchildren can prosper? First, we must own our anxieties and face our fears.

Here are three tips for troubled times: (1) Never forget that a coin has two sides. (2) Tune out financial fear-mongers (who are as clueless about the future as you and I). (3) Follow Buffett's example by keeping enough cash on hand for rainy *and* sunny days.

■ *Moral* ■

TRUST CASH ALWAYS.

BITE

No. 2

Trust CEOs Who Match Their Rhetoric with Their Record

Our long-avowed goal is to be the "buyer of choice" for businesses—particularly those built and owned by families. The way to achieve this goal is to deserve it. That means we must keep our promises; avoid leveraging up acquired businesses; grant unusual autonomy to our managers; and hold the purchased companies through thick and thin (though we prefer thick and thicker).

Our record matches our rhetoric. Most buyers competing against us follow a different path. For them, acquisitions are "merchandise." Before the ink dries on their purchase contracts, these operators are contemplating "exit strategies." We have a decided advantage, therefore, when we encounter sellers who truly care about the future of their businesses.

———

Buffett is rightly considered a great investor in mispriced stocks. He also wants to become "the buyer of choice" for businesses, particularly those built and owned by families. He's attracted to their cultures: the work ethic, discipline, pride of ownership, and reliable cash flow that come from homegrown enterprises. These are the same qualities that inspired Berkshire's evolution from a virtually bankrupt shirt manufacturing company to one of the largest and most respected companies in the world.

Owners of successful family businesses have often spent entire lifetimes creating valuable franchises. Would da Vinci have wanted a buyer of the *Mona Lisa* to tinker with that smile? Of course not. By the same token, these hard-working entrepreneurs don't want a new owner to mess with *their* masterpieces. Buffett knows that to achieve his goal of becoming the "buyer of choice" for family-owned businesses, he must (1) keep his promises, (2) avoid leveraging up acquired businesses, (3) grant unusual autonomy to his managers, and (4) hold onto the purchased companies through thick and thin. He's proud that Berkshire's "record matches our rhetoric."

This gives Buffett a competitive advantage. Many of his competitors treat acquisitions as merchandise to be traded like baseball cards. This attitude turns off business owners. The principles involved in wooing them are no different from those at play in a romantic courtship. They want to be loved for themselves first and their money second. (If the money comes first, then Buffett is not interested.) He wants CEOs who cherish their masterpieces and follow the golden rule when they work with their employees, investors, and customers.

■ *Moral* ■

THE GOLDEN RULE WORKS IN BUSINESS, TOO.

BITE

No. 3

Find CEOs Who Pick Outstanding Managers

Here is the record for the four legs to our insurance stool. The underwriting profits signify that all four provided funds to Berkshire last year without cost, just as they did in 2007. And in both years our underwriting profitability was considerably better than that achieved by the industry. . . .

Insurance Operations	Underwriting Profit (in millions)		Year-End Float	
	2008	2007	2008	2007
General Re	$ 342	$ 555	$21,074	$23,009
BH Reinsurance	1,324	1,427	24,221	23,692
GEICO	916	1,113	8,454	7,768
Other Primary	210	279	4,739	4,229
	$2,792	$3,374	$58,488	$58,698

Our insurance group has propelled Berkshire's growth since we first entered the business in 1967. This happy result has not been due to general prosperity in the industry. During the 25 years ending in 2007, return on net worth for insurers averaged 8.5% versus 14.0% for the Fortune 500. *Clearly our insurance CEOs have not had the wind at their back. Yet these managers have excelled to a degree Charlie and I never dreamed possible in the early days.* Why do I love them? Let me count the ways [emphasis added].

Unlike other insurance CEOs, Buffett provides a summary table in the shareholder letter that shows how his insurance businesses performed on two key scorecards: underwriting profit and year-end float. Recall that float is the cash received from policyholders that has yet to be paid in claims. Underwriting profit comes from taking the earnings from investing float and deducting insurance operating costs. The table on page 89 shows that Berkshire's insurance underwriting profits are down, just as Buffett had predicted they would be in his 2007 shareholder letter. At the same time, he tells us that Berkshire's 2008 profits beat the competition.

Importantly, all but one insurance division, General Re, grew its year-end float, and "all four provided funds to Berkshire last year without cost, just as they did in 2007." In response to this steady performance, Buffett turns his letter into a valentine as he counts the ways that he loves his insurance managers.

GREAT LEADERS NEVER UNDERESTIMATE
THE POWER OF WELL-DESERVED PRAISE.

BITE

No. 4

Rely on CEOs Who Nurture Healthy Corporate Cultures

Our two pipelines, Kern River and Northern Natural, were both acquired in 2002. A firm called Mastio regularly ranks pipelines for customer satisfaction. Among the 44 rated, Kern River came in 9th when we purchased it and Northern Natural ranked 39th. There was work to do. In Mastio's 2009 report, Kern River ranked 1st and Northern Natural 3rd. Charlie and I couldn't be more proud of this performance. It came about because *hundreds of people at each operation committed themselves to a new culture and then delivered on their commitment* [emphasis added].

Achievements at our electric utilities have been equally impressive. In 1995, MidAmerican became the major provider of electricity in Iowa. By judicious planning and a zeal for efficiency, the company has kept electric prices unchanged since our purchase and has promised to hold them steady through 2013. . . . MidAmerican has maintained this extraordinary price stability while making Iowa number one among all states in the percentage of its generation capacity that comes from wind. . . . Our partners in ownership of MidAmerican are its two terrific managers, Dave Sokol and Greg Abel, and my long-time friend, Walter Scott.

Berkshire's MidAmerican utilities business has four different business segments. In 2008, the pipelines segment reported the biggest gain in operating profit among all of the four—more than $100 million. It's now the second-largest segment in utilities. Buffett tells us how this happened: It was because "hundreds of people at each operation committed themselves to a new culture and delivered on their commitment."

Corporate culture—isn't this the soft stuff that hard-nosed analysts dismiss as unimportant? Yet Buffett says that culture change added $100 million to the pipeline segment's bottom line. What kinds of change is he talking about? He gives clues: improving customer satisfaction scores, a "zeal for efficiency," and efforts to keep prices low.

Corporate culture reveals the trustworthiness of financial statements. How so? Accounting numbers come from judgments that people make about when and how much cash to report. Their choices are shaped by corporate values and norms that a CEO can reinforce or subvert. Will accounting decisions in the companies you work for and invest in be prudent like Berkshire's or aggressive like Enron's? Check out the culture.

Moral

HEALTHY CULTURES CREATE WEALTH;
TOXIC CULTURES DESTROY IT.

Trust CEOs Who Count Losses When Analyzing Risks

Our third major insurance operation is Ajit Jain's reinsurance division, headquartered in Stamford and staffed by only 31 employees. This may be one of the most remarkable businesses in the world, hard to characterize but easy to admire.

From year to year, Ajit's business is never the same. It features very large transactions, incredible speed of execution and a willingness to quote on policies that leave others scratching their heads. When there is a huge and unusual risk to be insured, Ajit is almost certain to be called.

Ajit came to Berkshire in 1986. Very quickly, I realized that we had acquired an extraordinary talent. So I did the logical thing: I wrote his parents in New Delhi and asked if they had another one like him at home. Of course, I knew the answer before writing. There isn't anyone like Ajit. . . . *[W]e ourselves will periodically have a terrible year in insurance.* But, overall, I expect us to average an underwriting profit. If so, we will be using free funds of large size for the indefinite future [emphasis added].

Buffett writes that the Berkshire reinsurance division headed up by Ajit Jain is "hard to characterize but easy to admire." To appreciate what Jain and his band of reinsurers accomplished in 2008, consider this: In one year, Jain's 31-person shop accounted for $1.3 billion of Berkshire's underwriting profit, or roughly 47 percent of the total of Berkshire's insurance profits.

Buffett also reminds us that periodically Berkshire will have "a terrible year in insurance." This is inevitable because

Jain's business is highly volatile and involves potentially big risks. Reinsuring Lloyd's of London, hurricanes, and other unusual risks is the reason Berkshire keeps a lot of cash on hand—to pay out when one-time big insurance bets go against the company. So far it has not lost any bets, but Buffett has never soft-pedaled this eventuality. As long as he can profitably invest the billions of dollars of float that come from reinsurance, then *over time* this business will continue to be a winner.

▪ *Moral* ▪

TO CREATE LONG-LASTING WEALTH,
DON'T LOSE MONEY.

BITE

№ 6

Find CEOs Who Confess Their Mistakes

That's the good news. But there's another less pleasant reality: During 2008 I did some dumb things in investments. I made at least one major mistake of commission and several lesser ones that also hurt. I will tell you more about these later. Furthermore, I made some errors of omission, sucking my thumb when new facts came in that should have caused me to re-examine my thinking and promptly take action. . . .

[I] told you in an earlier part of this report that last year I made a major mistake of commission (and maybe more; this one sticks out). Without urging from Charlie or anyone else, I bought a large amount of ConocoPhillips stock when oil and gas prices were near their peak. I in no way anticipated the dramatic fall in energy prices that occurred in the last half of the year. I still believe the odds are good that oil sells far higher in the future than the current $40–$50 price. But so far I have been dead wrong. Even if prices should rise, moreover, the terrible timing of my purchase has cost Berkshire several billion dollars [emphasis added].

Buffett's investments don't always pan out. But you don't need an investigative journalist to have access to this news. Buffett openly admits to errors of both omission and commission in his letter. He tells us above that his terrible timing in purchasing ConocoPhillips when oil prices were peaking "has cost Berkshire several billion dollars." Not only does he take responsibility for "terrible timing," but he also reveals approximately how much this cost his shareholders. He makes fun of himself. Which other CEO admits to sucking his thumb instead of acting on new, important information?

Many of us were taught that confession is good for the soul, but most executives (and their lawyers) doubt that it is good for the bottom line. Still, can CEOs be truly transparent if they don't report their mistakes? Are CEOs supposed to be like superheroes, possessing special powers and infallible judgment? Perhaps this is how they justify their pay packages. But the last time I looked (figuratively speaking), CEOs put on their pants one leg at a time, just like the rest of us. They must make mistakes, but they almost never tell us about them.

Buffett shows us what he has learned from his mistake. As a result, we can hope that he will not do it again—and if he does, we trust he will tell us.

■ *Moral* ■

JUDGE CEOs ON THE QUALITY AND QUANTITY OF THEIR CONFESSIONS.

Find CEOs Who Understand Accounting

Now, let's take a look at the four major operating sectors of Berkshire. *Each of these has vastly different balance sheet and income account characteristics.* Therefore, lumping them together, as is done in standard financial statements, impedes analysis. So we'll present them as four separate businesses, which is how Charlie and I view them [emphasis added].

In order to better understand the wealth-producing advantages of his 67 businesses, Buffett chooses to evaluate them as four separate segments based on their "vastly different" financial reporting characteristics. These four segments are regulated utilities businesses; insurance; manufacturing, service, and retailing operations; and finance and financial products.

Then he does what no other CEO does: He prints the income statements and/or balance sheets of each of these four segments right in the body of his shareholder letter.

This is daunting to readers who have not taken Accounting 101, in which assets are always found on the left side of the accounting page and liabilities on the right. If you believe that accounting is as daunting as learning ancient Greek, then seeing these charts may cause heart palpitations, sweaty palms, and drowsiness. Buffett is sympathetic to the plight of the accounting-challenged. He often compares his lucid accounting explanations to eating spinach. It may not be what you want, but it sure is good for you.

A little patience brings great rewards. Not only will readers of Buffett's letter learn something important about each of Berkshire's businesses, but they can use their knowledge to understand how other companies create value.

When Buffett explains accounting, he puts on his teaching robes. He wants his investors to be informed, confident, and loyal.

Moral

AIDING INVESTORS' ANALYSIS BUILDS INVESTOR TRUST.

BITE

No. 8

Find Disciplined CEOs

As predicted in last year's report, the exceptional underwriting profits that our insurance businesses realized in 2007 were not repeated in 2008. Nevertheless, the insurance group delivered an underwriting gain for the sixth consecutive year. This means that our $58.5 billion of insurance "float"—money that doesn't belong to us but that we hold and invest for our own benefit—cost us less than zero. In fact, we were paid $2.8 billion to hold our float during 2008. Charlie and I find this enjoyable.

Over time, most insurers experience a substantial underwriting loss, which makes their economics far different from ours. Of course, we too will experience underwriting losses in some years.

But we have the best group of managers in the insurance business, and in most cases they oversee entrenched and valuable franchises. Considering these strengths, I believe that we will earn an underwriting profit over the years and that our float will therefore cost us nothing. Our insurance operation, the core business of Berkshire, is an economic powerhouse [emphasis added].

Everyone wants to know the secret of Buffett's success. The answer is simple: It's Berkshire's insurance business, an economic powerhouse. But before you run out to buy insurance company stocks, look more closely. The secret is not in the sector per se but in the float that insurance companies provide. Float is the cash received from the premiums paid by policyholders before claims are paid out. Buffett earns returns on this money before it is needed. Who wouldn't find it enjoyable to earn $2.8 billion simply for holding money?

This happy result is not magical. It happens because Buffett's insurance and investment managers are highly disciplined. This means these managers must write good contracts with good people, invest in sensible deals that fairly compensate Berkshire for assuming risk, and maintain healthy reserves to pay claims.

In my business, I've read shareholder letters from leading insurance CEOs over the past 10 years, and I have yet to find one that mentions the importance of float or underwriting discipline. Is this because these CEOs don't believe that float matters? We won't know. The recent experience at AIG shows why disciplined underwriting is vital to insurance company health—and to the health of the economy.

■ *Moral* ■

FAILED DISCIPLINE WILL LEAD TO A POORHOUSE,
NOT AN ECONOMIC POWERHOUSE.

BITE

No. 9

Trust CEOs Who Strengthen Competitive Positions

Most of the Berkshire businesses whose results are significantly affected by the economy earned below their potential last year, and that will be true in 2009 as well. Our retailers were hit particularly hard, as were our operations tied to residential construction. In aggregate, however, *our manufacturing, service and retail businesses earned substantial sums and most of them—particularly the larger ones—continue to strengthen their competitive positions*. Moreover, we are fortunate that Berkshire's two most important businesses—our insurance and utility groups—produce earnings that are not correlated to those of the general economy. Both businesses delivered outstanding results in 2008 and have excellent prospects.

In our insurance portfolios, we made three large investments on terms that would be unavailable in normal markets. These should add about $1½ billion pre-tax to Berkshire's annual earnings and offer possibilities for capital gains as well. . . . Additionally, certain of our subsidiaries made "tuck-in" acquisitions that will strengthen their competitive positions and earnings [emphasis added].

━━━

Because Buffett keeps loads of cash on hand for rainy days, he was able to make "three large investments on terms that would be unavailable in normal markets." Buffett likewise expects the managers of his 67 businesses to strengthen their competitive positions. He wants them to buy quality businesses and equipment at attractive, recession-reduced prices. These investments will "widen their moats" and help them grab more share of their markets. Moat building grows the cash that keeps Berkshire's mojo humming.

The global financial crisis inspires us to think about America's moat. Artificial means such as protectionist legislation or creative accounting aren't sustainable. Instead, we need to invest in real, honest-to-goodness services, products, and ideas that people around the world want to buy. What we offer has to be more innovative, economical, convenient, and reliable than anything else on the planet. And to increase sales, we must lower our drawbridges and stimulate a lot of two-way traffic.

Just like Buffett's businesses, the United States is earning less than its potential, but we are still earning substantial sums. How can these profits widen our moat?

■ *Moral* ■

REACH OUT IN A CRISIS; DON'T HUNKER DOWN.

How to Become an Intelligent Investor

*I make no attempt to forecast the general market—
my efforts are devoted to finding undervalued
securities. However, I do believe that wide-spread
public belief in the inevitability of profits from
investment in stocks will lead to eventual trouble.
Should this occur, prices, but not intrinsic values in
my opinion, of even undervalued securities can be
expected to be substantially affected.*

—WARREN E. BUFFETT,
1958 PARTNERSHIP LETTER,
FEBRUARY 11, 1959

BITE
No. 10

Ignore Sound Bites That Rattle Markets

In 75% of those years [from 1965 to 2008], the S&P stocks recorded a gain. I would guess that a roughly similar percentage of years will be positive in the next 44 [years]. But neither Charlie Munger, my partner in running Berkshire, nor I can predict the winning and losing years in advance. (In our usual opinionated view, we don't think anyone else can either.) We're certain, for example, that the economy will be in shambles throughout 2009—and, for that matter, probably well beyond—*but that conclusion does not tell us whether the stock market will rise or fall* [emphasis added].

113

Who can dispute that critical questioning and analysis are vital in a democracy? Today, however, independent thinking not only has grown scarce but is feared. Pundits tell us 24/7 what to think. They short-circuit and undermine our reasoning by selectively quoting from real thinkers.

A case in point is the release of Warren Buffett's 2008 shareholder letter on Saturday, February 28, 2009, and the havoc it created. Consider this frequently quoted and most misrepresented phrase from the fourth paragraph of the letter: "the economy will be in shambles throughout 2009 . . ."

Buffett's words spread quickly around the world via Internet postings, televised banner headlines, and print media. By the time the market closed on Monday, March 2, the S&P 500 index had fallen to its lowest point in two decades. It's impossible to say how much this quote contributed to the rout, but it surely did nothing to boost confidence.

Notice what the pundits left out after quoting "the economy will be in shambles": "does not tell us whether the stock market will rise or fall." Buffett reminds us that the economy and the market are like husband and wife—connected, but separate and different. Why was this concluding statement ignored? One reason is that pundits thrive on drama to boost ratings. But could they also fear a principle that turns their world upside down?

A CONCLUSION ABOUT THE ECONOMY
DOES NOT TELL US IF THE STOCK MARKET
WILL RISE OR FALL.

BITE

No. **11**

Treat Market Pessimism as Your Friend

Things also went well on the capital-allocation front last year. Berkshire is always a buyer of both businesses and securities, and the disarray in markets gave us a tailwind in our purchases. *When investing, pessimism is your friend, euphoria the enemy* [emphasis added].

What does Buffett mean by "capital-allocation front"? His term sounds like investment warfare. Indeed, Buffett sees his job not just as CEO but also as CCAO (Chief Capital Allocation Officer). He must make sure that Berkshire's cash is safe and that it works overtime to make more money for investors.

Like any great general, Buffett knows the value of surprise and time-tested principles. He has developed the mental toughness to treat market pessimism as his friend. When everyone else is heading for the hills, he chooses to deploy his capital. Rather than stuff money in mattresses and/or in the safety of U.S. Treasuries, Buffett searches for extraordinary opportunities.

The success of Buffett's campaign is easily measured. He wins the battle when he reinvests the cash generated by Berkshire's managers and, over time, the cash earns more than it cost. By keeping a sharp eye on cash costs and earned returns, Buffett has seen Berkshire's per-share book value increase at a 20.3 percent compounded rate over the past 45 years; that's over double the compounded rate of the S&P 500 during the same period.

Moral

GREAT CEOS NEED TO BE DISCIPLINED CAPITAL ALLOCATORS.

BITE

No. 12

Look Again If You Think the Sky Is Falling

Berkshire has two major areas of value. The first is our investments: stocks, bonds and cash equivalents. At yearend those totaled $122 billion (not counting the investments held by our finance and utility operations, which we assign to our second bucket of value). About $58.5 billion of that total is funded by our insurance float.

Berkshire's second component of value is earnings that come from sources other than investments and insurance. These earnings are delivered by our 67 non-insurance companies, itemized on page 96. We exclude our insurance earnings from this calculation because the value of our insurance operation comes from the investable funds it generates, and we have already included this factor in our first bucket.

In 2008, *our investments fell from $90,343 per share of Berkshire (after minority interest) to $77,793, a decrease that was caused by a decline in market prices, not by net sales of stocks or bonds.* Our second segment of value fell from pre-tax earnings of $4,093 per Berkshire share to $3,921 (again after minority interest). Both of these performances are unsatisfactory [emphasis added].

Buffett gets hit by market losses just like the rest of us. At year-end 2008, he reported that the value of Berkshire's per-share investment portfolio had dropped by 14 percent. It bears repeating. Buffett's portfolio is down just like ours. The smartest investor in the world shares our pain. This surprises people. If he is so smart, why is he losing money? The obvious answer is that he's human. But here's a more interesting question: What does Buffett do when his investments drop? Answer: He usually does nothing.

In his letter, Buffett writes that this decrease (in his portfolio) "was caused by a decline in market prices, not by net sales of stocks or bonds." The drop is a paper loss. Buffett knows that like the weather, markets will change. Inevitably his portfolio of quality stocks will rise again to plump up Berkshire's net worth. Buffett buys stocks and holds them. Whoever takes over Berkshire Hathaway will likely do the same. It's in the Berkshire DNA.

What if Buffett had panicked like Chicken Little when he was hit on the head by an acorn and thought the sky was falling? If Buffett had sold stocks at the bottom, Berkshire would have reported a real dollar loss. This would have produced some tax benefits and raised cash—but where would that cash have gone? Back into the stock market? Not a likely course of action when panic sets in. Berkshire shareholders are lucky that Buffett keeps his head: As the economy recovers, their fortunes will also improve.

■ *Moral* ■

AVOID THE CHICKEN LITTLE SYNDROME.

BITE

No. 13

Buy Quality Merchandise When It Is Marked Down

Additionally, the market value of the bonds and stocks that we continue to hold suffered a significant decline along with the general market. This does not bother Charlie and me. Indeed, we enjoy such price declines if we have funds available to increase our positions. *Long ago, Ben Graham taught me that "Price is what you pay; value is what you get."* Whether we're talking about socks or stocks, I like buying quality merchandise when it is marked down [emphasis added].

Buffett avoids the Chicken Little syndrome thanks to his Columbia University mentor Ben Graham, a brilliant teacher and investor and an exceptional human being. In his 1976 eulogy for Graham, Buffett wrote that his former professor and boss hoped each day to do "something foolish, something creative and something generous."

Graham, a value investor, invented the disciplines for analyzing stocks. Before Graham, Wall Street had no investing rules or principles. Buffett credits him with single-handedly bringing "logic and structure to a disorderly and confused activity." Among the greatest of these principles is: "Price is what you pay; value is what you get."

This value approach to investing has fallen out of favor in today's world of casino capitalism. Technological advances allow stock trading to pay off as quickly as the spin of a roulette wheel. But Buffett doesn't see companies as mere pieces of trading paper. He seeks to buy competitively advantaged businesses that he understands and that are run by trustworthy managers.

These qualities give Buffett the confidence to predict the lifetime cash flows from such a business. When he discounts these cash flows back to the present time, he determines the underlying intrinsic value of the business. Then he factors in a margin of safety. He buys stocks of good companies at prices below their per-share intrinsic value in order to improve his returns.

What is the intrinsic value of the home you own? In today's depressed market, is it worth more than you paid for it? If so, you bought wisely. But what if you had bought it at the market's peak? In today's slump, your investment would likely be below its intrinsic value. At Berkshire, value is measured against economic value, not speculative bubble prices.

❖ *Moral* ❖

PRICE IS WHAT YOU PAY;
VALUE IS WHAT YOU GET.

BITE

No. **14**

Don't Buy
$2,000 Cats

Clayton is the largest company in the manufactured home industry, delivering 27,499 units last year. This came to about 34% of the industry's 81,889 total. Our share will likely grow in 2009, partly because much of the rest of the industry is in acute distress. Industrywide, units sold have steadily declined since they hit a peak of 372,843 in 1998.

At that time, much of the industry employed sales practices that were atrocious. Writing about the period somewhat later, I described it as involving "borrowers who shouldn't have borrowed being financed by lenders who shouldn't have lent."

To begin with, the need for meaningful down payments was frequently ignored. Sometimes fakery was involved. ("That certainly looks like a $2,000 cat to me" says the salesman who will receive a $3,000 commission if the loan goes through.) Moreover, impossible-to-meet monthly payments were being agreed to by borrowers who signed up because they had nothing to lose. The resulting mortgages were usually packaged ("securitized") and sold by Wall Street firms to unsuspecting investors. This chain of folly had to end badly, and it did.

The image of a $2,000 cat is not easy to forget. It sounds ridiculous, and yet people who bought homes they could not keep, in effect, bought $2,000 cats. I bet today they might want to borrow at least one of a cat's nine lives. Perhaps they will remember next time around to compare the value of what they are buying with the price they are paying. They will then be less likely to succumb to the siren songs of commission-hungry salespeople. The same goes for people who were told that buying "securitized" bonds was a safe bet. Where are the credit default swap merchandisers who sold "insurance" to buyers who failed to ask why no reserves had been set aside?

As Buffett reminds us, a chain of folly will end badly. His warning evokes Aretha Franklin's solid gold hit "Chain of Fools," and is a haunting anthem for the great financial collapse of 2008.

■ *Moral* ■

A CHAIN OF FOLLY WILL ALWAYS END BADLY.

No. **15**

Put Your Money Where Your Home Is

Commentary about the current housing crisis often ignores the crucial fact that most foreclosures do not occur because a house is worth less than its mortgage (so-called upside-down loans). Rather, foreclosures take place because borrowers can't pay the monthly payment that they agreed to pay. Homeowners who have made a meaningful down payment—derived from savings and not from other borrowing—seldom walk away from a primary residence simply because its current value is less than the mortgage. Instead, they walk when they can't make the monthly payments.

Home ownership is a wonderful thing. My family and I have enjoyed my present home for 50 years, with more to come. But enjoyment and utility should be the primary motives for purchase, not profit or refi possibilities. And the home purchased ought to fit the income of the purchaser.

The present housing debacle should teach home buyers, lenders, brokers and government some simple lessons that will ensure stability in the future. Home purchases should involve an honest-to-God down payment of at least 10% and monthly payments that can be comfortably handled by the borrower's income. That income should be carefully verified. . . . Putting people into homes, though a desirable goal, shouldn't be our country's primary objective. Keeping them in their homes should be the ambition [emphasis added].

Fitting someone with a home and a mortgage needs to be done as carefully as fitting someone for a custom-made suit. The house payments need to match the size of the monthly income and the breadth of the future income stream. Buying a house is not like buying a lottery ticket.

It's a commitment. As Buffett points out, "enjoyment and utility" need to be the primary motivations for buying a house. There's no enjoyment in wondering how you're going to meet monthly mortgage payments that are beyond your means for a home that has crashed in value. Things happen that we cannot foresee. They always have and always will.

Charlie Munger, Berkshire's vice chair, once said, "Happiness is living beneath your means." This is much easier for him than for people who don't hold billions of dollars of Berkshire stock. But it's a good rule. Use it to budget your resources.

Buffett reminds us that the lesson learned from the housing crisis is simple: "Home purchases should involve an honest-to-God down payment of at least 10%." In addition, monthly house payments must be carefully verified by lenders and not overextend the family budget.

We need public policy that is geared to keeping people in their homes and avoiding future credit meltdowns. Home ownership is a desirable goal, but the only parties who benefit from putting people into homes they can't afford are fee-based mortgage brokers. To make sure the American dream doesn't turn into the American nightmare, home buyers need to understand the difference between speculating and investing in a home. Following Munger's advice will reduce stress and anxiety in the future, if not in the present.

■ *Moral* ■

LIVE BENEATH YOUR MEANS.

Master the Language of Business

Manufacturing, Service and Retailing Operations

Our activities in this part of Berkshire cover the waterfront. Let's look, though, at a summary balance sheet and earnings statement for the entire group.

Balance Sheet 12/31/08 (in millions)

Assets		Liabilities and Equity	
Cash and equivalents	$ 2,497	Notes payable	$ 2,212
Accounts and notes receivable	5,047	Other current liabilities	8,087
Inventory	7,500	Total current liabilities	10,299
Other current assets	752		
Total current assets	15,796		
Goodwill and other intangibles	16,515	Deferred taxes	2,786
Fixed assets	16,338	Term debt and other liabilities	6,033
Other assets	1,248	Equity	30,779
	$49,897		$49,897

Earnings Statement (in millions)

	2008	2007	2006
Revenues	$66,099	$59,100	$52,660
Operating expenses (including depreciation of $1,280 in 2008, $955 in 2007 and $823 in 2006)	61,937	55,026	49,002
Interest expense	139	127	132
Pre-tax earnings	4,023*	3,947*	3,526*
Income taxes and minority interests	1,740	1,594	1,395
Net income	$ 2,283	$ 2,353	$ 2,131

*Does not include purchase-accounting adjustments.

This motley group, which sells products ranging from lollipops to motor homes, earned an impressive 17.9% on average tangible net worth last year. It's also noteworthy that these operations used only minor financial leverage in achieving that return. Clearly we own some terrific businesses. *We purchased many of them, however, at large premiums to net worth—a point reflected in the goodwill item shown on our balance sheet—and that fact reduces the earnings on our average carrying value to 8.1%* [emphasis added].

Get ready for more spinach. In his report on Berkshire's manufacturing, service, and retailing operations, Buffett teaches us about the importance of goodwill.

Goodwill is an accounting term that describes the dollars paid to buy a business over and above its book value. In other words, goodwill is what's left after deducting liabilities (what a business owes) from its assets (what a business owns). Goodwill is a real number, but it tells us nothing about the future earning power of a business.

Buffett paid more for these businesses because he expects them to earn gobs of money in the future. In this happy event, the goodwill number is not relevant. However, if increased earnings don't materialize, the amount of goodwill will weigh on the earnings of a business.

Buffett tells us how this affects investor returns. By including the amount paid for goodwill in the return calculation, Buffett clearly reports the "cost" of goodwill. In 2008, Berkshire investors got a return of only 8.1 percent on their total net worth, including goodwill, compared to a return of 17.9 percent on tangible net worth, excluding goodwill.

No companies are required to report Buffett's level of detail and explain the cost of goodwill as Buffett does, even though most large U.S. companies have large amounts of goodwill reported on their balance sheets. This information is important to know. If companies pay more for acquisitions than the future earnings these ventures produce, investors will be harmed. Buffett is the only CEO I know who gives us this information. But then he would want this information if he were in our shoes.

■ *Moral* ■

GREAT LEADERS ARE GREAT TEACHERS.

BITE

No. 17

Do the Little Things Right

Though the full-year result was satisfactory, earnings of many of the businesses in this group hit the skids in last year's fourth quarter. Prospects for 2009 look worse. Nevertheless, the group retains strong earning power even under today's conditions and will continue to deliver significant cash to the parent company. Overall, these companies improved their competitive positions last year, partly because our financial strength let us make advantageous tuck-in acquisitions. In contrast, many competitors were treading water (or sinking).

MiTek, Benjamin Moore, Acme Brick, Forest River, Marmon and CTB also made one or more acquisitions during the year. CTB, which operates worldwide in the agriculture equipment field, has now picked up six small firms since we purchased it in 2002. At that time, we paid $140 million for the company. Last year its pre-tax earnings were $89 million. Vic Mancinelli, its CEO, followed Berkshire-like operating principles long before our arrival. *He focuses on blocking and tackling, day by day doing the little things right and never getting off course.* Ten years from now, Vic will be running a much larger operation and, more important, will be earning excellent returns on invested capital [emphasis added].

Buffett reports that Berkshire manufacturing, service, and retail businesses performed satisfactorily for the year. However, they hit the skids in fourth quarter 2008 because they depend on consumer confidence and spending. Still, Buffett is optimistic about their prospects. Berkshire's financial strength will allow these businesses to seize opportunities during this financial crisis. His business managers will be able to buy other businesses at what could be bargain prices.

Vic Mancinelli, CEO of CTB, an agricultural equipment company, one of Berkshire's boring manufacturing businesses, exemplifies another reason for optimism. In 2008, CTB earned $89 million. Since Buffett bought CTB in 2002, it has earned roughly an average 11 percent annual return, compared to the S&P return of only 3 percent. How can such a basic business produce eye-popping results? It wasn't through financial innovations or game-changing acquisitions. Instead, Mancinelli focused on "blocking and tackling, day by day doing the little things right and never getting off course." But slow and steady doesn't make headlines. Investors approaching the stock market continue to put their money on the hare, not the tortoise.

■ *Moral* ■

BETTING ON TORTOISES
CAN CREATE LONG-LASTING WEALTH.

BITE

№.18

Protect Your Capital When the Facts Turn Upside Down

Some years back our competitors were known as "leveraged-buyout operators." But LBO became a bad name. So in Orwellian fashion, the buyout firms decided to change their moniker. What they did not change, though, were the essential ingredients of their previous operations, including their cherished fee structures and love of leverage.

Their new label became *"private equity,"* a *name that turns the facts upside-down*: A purchase of a business by these firms almost invariably results in dramatic reductions in the equity portion of the acquiree's capital structure compared to that previously existing. A number of these acquirees, purchased only two to three years ago, are now in mortal danger because of the debt piled on them by their private-equity buyers. Much of the bank debt is selling below 70¢ on the dollar, and the public debt has taken a far greater beating. The private-equity firms, it should be noted, are not rushing in to inject the equity their wards now desperately need. Instead, they're keeping their remaining funds very private [emphasis added].

George Orwell, in his book *1984* (published in 1949), described a frightening future in which the government controlled the minds of its citizens. It forced everyone to repeatedly shout slogans like "freedom is slavery" and "ignorance is strength." Yet, Buffett notes, this cognitive dissonance is no more absurd than the term "private equity."

Think about it. Why call people who buy public companies with massive amounts of debt "private equity investors"? A more accurate label would be "investors who raise a lot of debt and put in as little equity as they can in order to take control of public companies." Remember, debt capital is far cheaper than equity. When times get tough, debt investors get paid before equity investors get paid.

But like people who bought homes with too much debt during the credit bubble, private equity investors overleveraged the companies they took private. Buffett reports that the bank debt of these troubled companies has sold "below 70¢ on the dollar," and that the market price of debt that is still held by the public "has taken a far greater beating."

With more than a hint of disgust, Buffett notes that instead of injecting their own money to support these troubled companies, these debt-addicted owners keep their funds "very private." Rather than act like owners, they act like renters.

Not so long ago, private equity moguls were called "leveraged buyout operators." Before that, they were known as "corporate raiders." It's lucky for Berkshire that Buffett never got dazzled by these linguistic acrobatics that were repeated unquestioningly by the media.

■ *Moral* ■

ORWELLIAN SHENANIGANS CAN TIP US OFF
TO FINANCIAL SHENANIGANS.

BITE
No. 19

Imagine a Pendulum

The investment world has gone from under-pricing risk to overpricing it. This change has not been minor; the pendulum has covered an extraordinary arc. A few years ago, it would have seemed unthinkable that yields like today's could have been obtained on good-grade municipal or corporate bonds even while risk-free governments offered near-zero returns on short-term bonds and no better than a pittance on long-terms. When the financial history of this decade is written, it will surely speak of the Internet bubble of the late 1990s and the housing bubble of the early 2000s. But the U.S. Treasury bond bubble of late 2008 may be regarded as almost equally extraordinary.

Clinging to cash equivalents or long-term government bonds at present yields is almost certainly a terrible policy if continued for long. Holders of these instruments, of course, have felt increasingly comfortable—in fact, almost smug—in following this policy as financial turmoil has mounted. They regard their judgment confirmed when they hear commentators proclaim "cash is king," even though that wonderful cash is earning close to nothing and will surely find its purchasing power eroded over time.

Approval, though, is not the goal of investing. In fact, approval is often counter-productive because it sedates the brain and makes it less receptive to new facts or a re-examination of conclusions formed earlier. Beware the investment activity that produces applause; the great moves are usually greeted by yawns.

Two contrasting images capture the workings of financial markets. One is the spiking and dipping EKG line that plots the heart's electrical activity. This line resembles a stock trading chart, showing high and low prices over time. A different image, favored by Buffett, is a pendulum. He observes that over the last few years, the market has "covered an extraordinary arc" and swung from "under-pricing risk to significantly overpricing it."

In late 2008, investors, spooked by an unstable stock market, were putting more of their money into "safe" Treasury securities. Demand for short-term Treasury paper was so great that returns approached zero and longer-term bonds offered a mere pittance. This rush to safety drove down prices and bid up yields on good-grade municipal and corporate bonds. Financial historians, Buffett noted, will record this "U.S. Treasury bond bubble" as the equal of other recent bubbles.

Ignoring the trend to buy Treasury securities and hoard cash, Buffett bought quality investments that were underpriced in this bubble. He warns that it is risky to seek approval for our investing strategies; this can sedate our brains. He expects his moves to produce yawns.

■ *Moral* ■

WHAT LOOKS SAFE MAY BE UNSAFE: CHALLENGE
ASSUMPTIONS AND BE OPEN TO NEW FACTS.

BITE

№20

Question History-Based Models

Investors should be skeptical of history-based models. Constructed by a nerdy-sounding priesthood using esoteric terms such as beta, gamma, sigma and the like, these models tend to look impressive. Too often, though, investors forget to examine the assumptions behind the symbols. Our advice: Beware of geeks bearing formulas.

Can we blame Shakespeare for the global economic collapse? In *The Tempest* he wrote, "[W]hat's past is prologue." He affirms a view that the past shapes and even determines our present circumstances. This powerful idea is engraved on the outside of the National Archives Building in Washington, D.C. With such legitimacy, it is hard to fault CEOs and investment bankers who develop new investing strategies and financial products based on past experience. But Buffett urges us to question these history-based models. He warns that blindly relying on the past to predict the future can be a ticket to the poorhouse.

Massive losses in mortgage-backed securities occurred when rating agencies, investors, and financial salespeople unthinkingly relied on history. They looked back to a time when "home prices rose only moderately and speculation in houses was negligible." Then they projected these past foreclosure rates onto current experience that was quite different: Prices for new homes in 2006 and 2007 had risen to speculative levels, loan standards had deteriorated, and many buyers had purchased homes they could not afford. "In short," writes Buffett, "universe 'past' and universe 'current' had very different characteristics. But lenders, government and media largely failed to recognize this all-important fact."

Geeks (including Nobel Prize–winning economists) who develop statistically valid, back-tested financial models to support the invention of new securities often fail to examine basic assumptions. These creators of history-based models are advised to consider the full import of Shakespeare's quote: "Whereof what's past is prologue, what['s] to come [is] in yours and my discharge."

BEWARE OF GEEKS BEARING FORMULAS.

Derivatives Are Dangerous

Derivatives are dangerous. They have dramatically increased the leverage and risks in our financial system. They have made it almost impossible for investors to understand and analyze our largest commercial banks and investment banks. They allowed Fannie Mae and Freddie Mac to engage in massive misstatements of earnings for years. So indecipherable were Freddie and Fannie that their federal regulator, OFHEO, whose more than 100 employees had no job except the oversight of these two institutions, totally missed their cooking of the books.

A derivative is a financial contract that requires the exchange of money at some future date. The amount to be exchanged is derived from a predetermined measure, such as the value of shares of stock, an index, commodities, bonds, and currencies. In other words, derivatives allow financial experts to trade securities that are based on the value of something related to an asset, not the asset itself. This flexibility inspires financial innovation.

In his 2002 letter, Buffett rang alarm bells, calling derivatives "financial weapons of mass destruction." He announced that he was unwinding a portfolio of 23,218 derivatives contracts that he had inherited in the 1998 acquisition of giant reinsurer General Re. No one forced Buffett to do this. He simply did not want to own what he could not understand. Shedding this portfolio was no walk in the park.

Five years later and at a cost of more than $400 million, Buffett announced in his 2006 shareholder letter that he had largely completed the task. He succeeded because of the generous credit terms and liquid markets that prevailed during this time. Buffett warned that it would have been nearly impossible to do this in a credit-scarce environment. Paraphrasing Shakespeare he noted, "All's Well that Ends."

After these dire warnings, readers might well be shocked to learn that Buffett reports in this same letter that he has 251 derivative contracts still outstanding. Recognizing the apparent hypocrisy of these investment choices, he reassures readers that (1) each of the contracts was mispriced and will add value in the future; (2) he personally manages the contracts, including counterparty risk; and (3) each contract has a clearly defined metric to determine future value. Whether or not this disclosure satisfies you, can you name one other CEO who clearly states how the derivatives under his watch meet measurable criteria?

■ *Moral* ■

Invest with CEOs

WHO EXPLAIN IMPORTANT RISKS.

BITE

No. 22

What You Can't See Can Still Bite You

A normal stock or bond trade is completed in a few days with one party getting its cash, the other its securities. Counterparty risk therefore quickly disappears, which means credit problems can't accumulate. This rapid settlement process is key to maintaining the integrity of markets. That, in fact, is a reason for NYSE and NASDAQ shortening the settlement period from five days to three days in 1995.

Derivatives contracts, in contrast, often go unsettled for years, or even decades, with counterparties building up huge claims against each other. "Paper" assets and liabilities—often hard to quantify—become important parts of financial statements though these items will not be validated for many years. Additionally, a frightening web of mutual dependence develops among huge financial institutions. Receivables and payables by the billions become concentrated in the hands of a few large dealers who are apt to be highly-leveraged in other ways as well. Participants seeking to dodge troubles face the same problem as someone seeking to avoid venereal disease: It's not just whom you sleep with, but also whom they are sleeping with.

In his 2002 shareholder letter, Buffett noted that General Re's derivative contracts involved 884 counterparties, the entities at the other end of his derivative contracts. Because these derivative contracts take a long time to settle, unanticipated events can have a negative impact on the relationship between the issuer and the counterparties. For example, in the event that derivative issuers get into credit trouble, they are required to add collateral in order to support the transaction. Buffett equates this collateral call risk to a time bomb.

This risk exploded on April 3, 2008, when Tim Geithner, who was then the president of the New York Fed, explained the need to rescue Bear Stearns: "The sudden discovery by Bear's derivative counterparties that important financial positions they had put in place to protect themselves from financial risk were no longer operative would have triggered substantial further dislocation in markets. This would have precipitated a rush by Bear's counterparties to liquidate the collateral they held against those positions and to attempt to replicate those positions in already very fragile markets." Buffett translates this Fedspeak as, "We stepped in to avoid a financial chain reaction of unpredictable magnitude."

Buffett notes how companies that slept around and accumulated significant counterparty risks were quick to gain government aid. He concludes: "From this irritating reality comes The First Law of Corporate Survival for ambitious CEOs who pile on leverage and run large and unfathomable derivatives books: Modest incompetence simply won't do; it's mindboggling screw-ups that are required."

▪ *Moral* ▪

REMEMBER THAT LARGE, UNFATHOMABLE
DERIVATIVES ARE STILL FINANCIAL
WEAPONS OF MASS DESTRUCTION.

BITE
No. 23

Seek Simplicity
and Candor

Improved "transparency"—a favorite remedy of politicians, commentators and financial regulators for averting future train wrecks—won't cure the problems that derivatives pose. I know of no reporting mechanism that would come close to describing and measuring the risks in a huge and complex portfolio of derivatives. Auditors can't audit these contracts, and regulators can't regulate them. When I read the pages of "disclosure" in 10-Ks of companies that are entangled with these instruments, all I end up knowing is that I don't know what is going on in their portfolios (and then I reach for some aspirin).

The word "transparency" comes from the Latin *parere* and means "to be easily understood or seen through." In contrast, the word "candor" is derived from *candere*, meaning "to shine." It is defined as "the quality of being honest and straightforward in attitude and speech." This deeper definition, grounded in behavior, is the reason we measure CEO candor in our surveys, not transparency. It is not enough to appear to be clear; we need CEOs to deliver substance. We want them to tell us what they know—and don't know.

But regulators, pundits, market reformers, and corporate activists have a different view. They cite transparency as a cure-all for market shenanigans. Not so, says Buffett. Reading corporate footnotes and the fine print of derivatives offerings is too often an exercise in futility. If Warren Buffett and Charlie Munger cannot understand these disclosures, then what can we expect from investors and analysts who lack their financial I.Q.s? How can regulators be expected to monitor them?

In the aftermath of the global financial crisis, it is difficult to find anyone who admits they understood the fine print in credit default swaps. And yet billions of dollars of these securities were sold. Perhaps it is the duty of regulators to tell us when a transaction is too complex.

Like the little boy who shouted that the emperor had no clothes, Buffett seems alone when he cries that the complexity of derivatives systems is virtually impossible to describe.

▪ *Moral* ▪

INDECIPHERABLE DISCLOSURES TELL US WHICH EMPERORS ARE NAKED.

BITE

No. 24

Remember That We Are All in the Same Boat

The table on the preceding page [pages 43–44 of this book], recording both the 44-year performance of Berkshire's book value and the S&P 500 Index, shows that 2008 was the worst year for each. The period was devastating as well for corporate and municipal bonds, real estate and commodities. By yearend, investors of all stripes were bloodied and confused, much as if they were small birds that had strayed into a badminton game.

Whatever the downsides may be, strong and immediate action by government was essential last year if the financial system was to avoid a total breakdown. Had one occurred, the consequences for every area of our economy would have been cataclysmic. *Like it or not, the inhabitants of Wall Street, Main Street and the various Side Streets of America were all in the same boat* [emphasis added].

Comparing derivatives to "weapons of financial mass destruction" is a haunting image, especially for those who live near the vast hole where the Twin Towers were, the folks who worked at the Pentagon, the families of loved ones in the doomed planes—and all Americans. Do you remember how the horror of 9/11 united people around the world? The actions of everyday heroes inspired us to see how tightly our human destinies are intertwined.

Of course, there is a difference. After the attacks, we united as a country against a common enemy from outside. Today's economic tragedy is tougher to face because the financial terror we fear was perpetrated by people inside our own system who were allowed to play by their own rules. They were aided by others who remained silent. They did not speak out. Many of these people are our neighbors and friends.

Today we are facing financial devastation. We feel like Buffett's "bloodied and confused" small battered birds. Where is the steady ground we can plant our feet on? Buffett reminds us of an inescapable truth: "[T]he inhabitants of Wall Street, Main Street and the various Side Streets of America" are all in the same boat. And if this boat is to reach the safety of land, we must defend the rule of law, hope for redemption, and pull together.

■ *Moral* ■

RECOVERY DEPENDS ON CHOOSING
TO RESTORE OUR SOCIAL COMPACT AND TO
RESET OUR MORAL COMPASSES.

BITE

No. 25

When You Fall Down, Get Up Again

Amid this bad news, however, never forget that our country has faced far worse travails in the past. In the 20th century alone, we dealt with two great wars (one of which we initially appeared to be losing); a dozen or so panics and recessions; virulent inflation that led to a 21½% prime rate in 1980; and the Great Depression of the 1930s, when unemployment ranged between 15% and 25% for many years. America has had no shortage of challenges.

Without fail, however, we've overcome them. In the face of those obstacles—and many others— the real standard of living for Americans improved nearly seven-fold during the 1900s, while the Dow

Jones Industrials rose from 66 to 11,497. Compare the record of this period with the dozens of centuries during which humans secured only tiny gains, if any, in how they lived. Though the path has not been smooth, our economic system has worked extraordinarily well over time. It has unleashed human potential as no other system has, and it will continue to do so. *America's best days lie ahead* [emphasis added].

How can Buffett be so sure that our best days lie ahead? He's often told us that he lacks a crystal ball. But he *chooses* to believe this. And because he does, it is more likely that *his* best days lie ahead.

Those of us who don't subscribe to the power of positive thinking may be skeptical. When Americans faced the Great Depression and past inflations, our country was still a nation defined by the values of hard work, fair play, square deals, reasoned discourse, and doing the right thing. Our current crisis has been brought on by our doomed love affair with easy money, our fascination with casino capitalism, and the failed accountability of trusted leaders. All this experience has undermined our bedrock values. Will Americans return to the values that made us great?

An astute Canadian investor I know is betting on us, on the United States. Why? Americans are a resilient people. We fall down and get up again. We live in a nation built on impossible dreams. We are the sons and daughters of courageous, visionary leaders and revolutionary soldiers like those who fought at the Battle of Trenton. Without pay and shoes, cold and wet, these patriots crossed the Delaware River on a dark, stormy Christmas Day. They marched in blinding snow, their bare feet bloodied, to fight mercenaries with superior weapons and warm food. What sustained them? It sure wasn't the money. Buffett gives us a hint.

■ *Moral* ■

THEY FOUGHT FOR SELF-EVIDENT TRUTHS.

Principles-Based Capitalism for the Twenty-First Century

Fiduciary Genetics:
The Berkshire Hathaway Owner's Manual

> *It's not that CEOs are unprincipled people. It's that*
> *they lack principles about shareholders; they'd have a*
> *hard time writing an Owner's Manual.*
>
> —2002 INTERVIEW WITH WARREN BUFFETT

A principle is defined as "a rule or standard especially of good behavior or a basic truth, law or assumption as in the principles of democracy." In order to create a democracy based on self-governing authority, the American founding fathers set out bold new principles respecting self-evident truths. For more than two centuries, these principles have been tested in wars, depressions, and terrorist attacks; they continue to inspire people around the world.

Buffett wrote the Berkshire Hathaway Owner's Manual in 1999. It is his Declaration of Partner-Based Capitalism, a codification of principles that link respect for investors' rights with economically sound capital allocation practices. Initially the Owner's Manual was printed as a separate document, but now it is included in the Berkshire Hathaway annual report. (It is also easily downloaded from the Internet.) Buffett wants investors to read the Manual in connection with his shareholder letters—but practically no one does.

When I ask people about the Owner's Manual, I usually get a blank stare.

Once when I asked Buffett why more CEOs didn't write an owner's manual, he said, "They'd have a hard time writing it, and in the end it doesn't make them wealthier. It's like Charlie said, 'We got the fiduciary gene, not the Mother Teresa gene.'"

Fiduciaries and Executive Privilege

A fiduciary is defined as an "individual or institution that has a legal and ethical duty to act in the best interests of another party." Bound by law, a fiduciary is obliged to put aside personal interests and act in good faith when making decisions for the benefit of others.

Buffett's sense of duty comes from his father, Howard Buffett. In 1942 the elder Buffett was elected to the U.S. Congress, representing the Omaha congressional district. Not long after he arrived in Washington, his fellow legislators voted to increase their own salaries. Congressman Buffett turned down his increase. Why? He said that he would keep the lower salary that was in effect when he was elected. This was the deal he had struck with his voters. He would honor it.

Buffett observes the same spirit when he looks after his shareowners' interests. He wants to avoid confrontations reminiscent of the ugly standoff in 1215 between greedy King John of England and his heavily taxed barons. Cornered at Runnymede, the king was forced to write down rules that limited his powers. For the first time in human history, a written contract, the Magna Carta, reined in executive privilege. Buffett's Berkshire Hathaway Owner's Manual is his Magna Carta. It spells out what investors can expect when they become Berkshire owners.

Here is a summary of the 11 principles from this Manual that have been cited in other chapters. As you review them, consider that finding similar ones at other companies is about as rare as locating a trap door on a lifeboat.

Review of Owner's Manual Principles

1. Although our form is corporate, our attitude is partnership.

2. In line with Berkshire's owner orientation, most of our directors have a major portion of their net worth invested in the company. We eat our own cooking.

3. Our long-term economic goal (subject to some qualifications mentioned later) is to maximize Berkshire's average annual rate of gain in intrinsic business value on a per-share basis.

4. Our preference would be to reach our [long-term economic] goal by directly owning a diversified group of businesses that generate cash and consistently earn above-average returns on capital.

5. Charlie and I both as owners and managers virtually ignore such consolidated [reported earnings] . . . we will try to give you in the annual report the numbers and other information that really matter.

6. Accounting consequences do not influence our operating or capital-allocation decisions.

7. See below.

8. A managerial "wish list" will not be filled at shareholder expense.

9. We test the wisdom of retaining earnings by assessing whether retention, over time, delivers shareholders at least $1 of market value for each $1 retained.

10. We will issue common stock only when we receive as much in business value as we give.

11. See below.

12. We will be candid in our reporting to you, emphasizing the pluses and minuses important in appraising business value. . . . The CEO who misleads others in public may eventually mislead himself in private.

13. Despite our policy of candor, we will discuss our activities in marketable securities only to the extent legally required.

We have not yet considered principles 7 and 11. They are outliers. In principle 7, Buffett informs investors that he will keep relatively low levels of debt and high levels of cash at Berkshire. In principle 11, he reports that he does not intend to sell any of Berkshire's businesses. Both principles tell us how far Buffett is willing to go to trade a few extra profit points for a good night's sleep.

Use Debt Sparingly

Over the past decade, investors have lurched from bubble to bubble. The pattern is unmistakable: The U.S. economy is bulimic. Certain industry sectors—first technology, then energy, and most recently housing—have gorged on huge amounts of debt. Inevitably the time comes when it is necessary to expel the unhealthy excesses brought on by these binges. It is never a pretty sight.

Buffett's antidote to debt bingeing lies in principle 7 of his Owner's Manual: "We use debt sparingly, and when we do borrow, we attempt to structure our loans on a long-term fixed-rate basis. We will reject interesting opportunities rather than over-leverage our balance sheet." He readily admits, however, that this "conservatism has penalized our results."

What is this penalty? Buffett describes how many companies often add a lot of debt and overleverage their corporate balance sheets. They indulge in these practices because debt capital is less expensive than equity. The reason is that debt holders are paid before equity holders when a company gets into financial trouble.

If Buffett added more debt, he would reduce Berkshire's cost of capital and simplify his job as chief capital allocation officer. With a lower cost of capital, he could consider a greater number of new investments that earn at or above the new lower cost of capital. With cheaper money, Buffett could also afford to pay more for investments. But overleveraging also increases risk. It weakens fiscal discipline and can jeopardize corporate reputations. When money gets tight, fearful lenders will not invest in overleveraged companies. Without ready cash, bankruptcy protection may become the only option.

Buffett fiercely guards Berkshire's reputation. While the dollar value of corporate reputation isn't reported in the financial statements, it may well be the company's most valuable asset. Because of his trusted reputation and cash-fortified balance sheet, Buffett gets to see transactions that others do not. People respect his judgment and are confident that they can rely on his discretion. Buffett is decisive and makes bankable promises. He first cements deals with a handshake and then brings in the lawyers to draw up agreements.

Words and promises matter a great deal to Buffett. He tells Berkshire's insurance customers that he will always pay their claims promptly. He promises debt holders that he will make timely interest and principal payments. He assures his owner-partners that he will maintain their equity values. The preservation of Berkshire's reputation requires that he honor these commitments in rising *and* falling markets. It lets him sleep at night. He explains: "I've never believed in risking what my family and friends have and need in order to pursue what they don't have and don't need."

But investors who play the market according to casino rules are quick to sign up for extra points of return. They forget that markets are prone to earthquake-like risk. They forget that Cinderella's ball must end—and that the clock they are watching has no hands. They neglect one of Buffett's most valuable tips: When you are promised consistently high investment returns, look to see how much comes from debt leverage. It *is* possible to have too much of a good thing.

Avoid Gin Rummy Behavior

Another Buffett belief that reduces Berkshire's returns is spelled out in principle 11: "Regardless of price, we have no interest at all in selling any good businesses that Berkshire owns." Buffett states that he is also "very reluctant to sell sub-par businesses as long as we expect them to generate at least some cash and as long as we feel good about their managers and labor relations." In other words, he will not play gin rummy with the companies he owns. He won't "*discard* [the] *least promising business at each turn.*"

This is corporate finance heresy. Why would he refuse to sell any of his businesses? Sure, most CEOs are unlikely to sell profitable businesses, but why would they keep ones that are sub-par? For Buffett, it is necessary to maintain trust. He assures owners who become part of the Berkshire family that he buys for life. By keeping his word, Buffett inspires other interested sellers to write and tempt him with their quality businesses. Trust is the grease that keeps the Berkshire cash machine churning. Never forget that Buffett similarly expects Berkshire's investors to hold, not flip, their stock. As a result, he will not discard the businesses of owners who sell their companies to him.

Twenty-First-Century Brains

The Owner's Manual principles are based on Buffett's respect for human contradictions. He accepts the fact that our neural wiring makes us unpredictable, inconsistent, illogical, and emotional. We can be greedy and generous, loving and hateful, fearful and courageous, sometimes from moment to moment. In dealing with financial markets we are both rational and irrational.

When faced with volatile financial markets, we act irrationally. We rejoice as markets rise to new heights, even though we should be fearful. We panic as market prices fall to new lows and shout "Sell" when we should be screaming "Buy!" Berkshire's wealth record is based on Buffett's ability to override this neural wiring. This is the genius of the Owner's Manual principles: They instill patience. They short-circuit our impulsive instinctual responses.

By following the Owner's Manual principles, Berkshire maintains stable cash flows that can be invested in falling markets. Rather than relying on complex, costly reporting rules and penalties to protect shareholder rights, Buffett defines the behaviors that lead to shareholder-friendly governance. And by walking his talk, he builds a trustworthy enterprise.

Buffett's dedication to his principles has turned him into a financial folk hero. Yet despite his celebrity status, the Berkshire model is still not widely accepted as the gold standard to be followed by corporate directors, CEOs, large influential investors, and government policymakers. Berkshire is an outlier, a business anomaly. Critics diminish Buffett's innovations. They say he is not an entrepreneur like Microsoft's Bill Gates. They just don't get it.

Warren Buffett and Galileo:
Traditions of Heresy

It is ridiculous ... the way a lot of people cling to failed ideas. Keynes said, "It's not bringing in the new ideas that's so hard. It's getting rid of the old ones."

—CHARLES T. MUNGER, *POOR CHARLIE'S ALMANACK*

An entrepreneur is an individual who identifies opportunities and exploits them. Such people are driven by a need to innovate or invent something that can disrupt the status quo.

Critics who complain that Buffett has not created anything new may be forgiven for their shortsightedness.

Buffett's innovations are not the same as offering the next edition of Microsoft Office. Instead, he offers a working model of a principles-based company. The foundation of his edifice is built on (1) intelligently allocating capital for long-term wealth and (2) following the golden rule of owner-partner capitalism.

Buffett's principles defy conventional capitalism. Like Galileo, who believed that the sun—not the earth—was the center of the universe, Buffett puts ownership and stewardship, not greed, at Berkshire's core. Still, people doubt his creation. The financial establishment, in particular, is reluctant to embrace owner-partner, principles-based capitalism.

Munger tells a story about a professor who taught the Buffett and Graham principles at one of the most prestigious business schools in the United States. This professor's classes were always oversubscribed. He was frequently voted the most popular teacher by the students. And yet some people couldn't wait for him to retire. Make no mistake, Warren Buffett, the affable, joke-cracking financial wizard, is a troublemaker. His shareholder letters, particularly since the late 1990s, are indictments of corporate shenanigans.

Defying Conventional Wisdom: Efficient Market Theory

Buffett scoffs at the idea that markets are always efficient. This may be true over the long term, but certainly not in the short term. And yet, this is what business students are led to believe. In his 2006 letter, Buffett describes the amazing record of legendary investor Walter Schloss to illustrate the wrongheadedness of efficient market theory (EMT):

Let me end this section by telling you about one of the good guys of Wall Street, my long-time friend Walter Schloss, who last year turned 90. From 1956 to 2002, Walter managed a remarkably successful investment partnership, from which he took not a dime unless his investors made money. My admiration for Walter, it should be noted, is not based on hindsight. A full fifty years ago, Walter was my sole recommendation to a St. Louis family who wanted an honest and able investment manager.

Walter did not go to business school, or for that matter, college. His office contained one file cabinet in 1956; the number mushroomed to four by 2002. Walter worked without a secretary, clerk or bookkeeper, his only associate being his son, Edwin, a graduate of the North Carolina School of the Arts. Walter and Edwin never came within a mile of inside information. Indeed, they used "outside" information only sparingly, generally selecting securities by certain simple statistical methods Walter learned while working for Ben Graham. When Walter and Edwin were asked in 1989 by *Outstanding Investors Digest*, "How would you summarize your approach?" Edwin replied, "We try to buy stocks cheap." So much for Modern Portfolio Theory, technical analysis, macroeconomic thoughts and complex algorithms.

Following a strategy that involved no real risk—defined as permanent loss of capital—Walter produced results over his 47 partnership years that dramatically surpassed those of the S&P 500. It's particularly noteworthy that he built this record by investing in about 1,000 securities, mostly of a lackluster type. A few big winners did not account for his success. It's safe to say that had millions of investment managers made trades by a) drawing stock names from a hat; b) purchasing these stocks in comparable amounts when Walter made a purchase; and then c) selling when Walter sold his pick, the *luckiest* of them would not have come close to equaling his record. There is simply no possibility that what Walter achieved over 47 years was due to chance.

I first publicly discussed Walter's remarkable record in 1984. At that time "efficient market theory" (EMT) was the centerpiece of investment instruction at most major business schools. This theory, as then most commonly taught, held that the price of any stock at any moment is not demonstrably mispriced, which means that no investor can be *expected* to overperform the stock market averages using only publicly-available information (though some will do so by luck). When I talked about Walter 23 years ago, his record forcefully contradicted this dogma.

And what did members of the academic community do when they were exposed to this new and important evidence? Unfortunately, they reacted in all-too-human fashion: Rather than opening their minds, they closed their eyes. To my knowledge *no* business school teaching EMT made any attempt to study Walter's performance and what it meant for the school's cherished theory.

Instead, the faculties of the schools went merrily on their way presenting EMT as having the certainty of scripture. Typically, a finance instructor who had the nerve to question EMT had about as much chance of major promotion as Galileo had of being named Pope.

Tens of thousands of students were therefore sent out into life believing that on every day the price of every stock was "right" (or, more accurately, not demonstrably wrong) and that attempts to evaluate businesses—that is, stocks—were useless. Walter meanwhile went on overperforming, his job made easier by the misguided instructions that had been given to those young minds. After all, if you are in the shipping business, it's helpful to have all of your potential competitors be taught that the earth is flat.

Maybe it was a good thing for his investors that Walter didn't go to college.

This critique only hints at the extent of Buffett's beef with corporate orthodoxy. Consider his tirades against excessive CEO compensation and his preference for business owners who, like artists, create business masterpieces because they love what they do.

The Battle of Excessive CEO Compensation

In each of his shareholder letters from 2002 to 2007, Buffett has complained about excessive CEO compensation. Remember that he has asked his board to pay him only $100,000 a year—indefinitely. In his 2002 shareholder letter, he challenged boards of directors to exercise their fiduciary duties on behalf of the owners they are charged to represent:

In the 1890s, Samuel Gompers described the goal of organized labor as "More!" In the 1990s, America's CEOs adopted his battle cry. The upshot is that CEOs have often amassed riches while their shareholders have experienced financial disasters.

Directors should stop such piracy. There's nothing wrong with paying well for truly exceptional business performance. But, for anything short of that, it's time for directors to shout "Less!" It would be a travesty if the bloated pay of recent years became a baseline for future compensation. Compensation committees should go back to the drawing boards.

In his 2003 shareholder letter, Buffett took on the compensation consultants who are hired to advise corporate directors on CEO compensation. He questioned how consultants hired by the CEO could ever establish pay packages that were fair to shareholders. This was an unequal negotiation in which owners would always lose. Charlie Munger felt even more strongly about this issue, saying once that he "would rather throw a viper down my shirt front than hire a compensation consultant."

In his 2004 letter, Buffett criticized the practice of granting stock options as part of CEO compensation and failing to report this as a legitimate business expense:

While we are on the subject of self-interest, let's turn again to the most important accounting mechanism still available to CEOs who wish to overstate earnings, the non-expensing of stock options. The accomplices in perpetuating this absurdity have been many members of Congress who have defied the arguments put forth by all the Big Four auditors, all members of the Financial Accounting Standards Board and virtually all investment professionals.

———

Buffett says that to believe that stock options should not be expensed is ostrich-like nonsense. Stock options are paid to compensate executives. Since compensation is a deductible expense, why *wouldn't* stock options also be deducted? Over the years, CEOs compounded this nonsense by paying lobbyists (with shareholder dollars) to keep Congress from passing laws that would mandate stock option expensing.

In his 2005 letter, Buffett noted that CEO pay had increasingly less to do with performance and results:

———

Getting fired can produce a particularly bountiful payday for a CEO. Indeed, he can "earn" more in that single day, while cleaning out his desk, than an American worker earns in a lifetime of cleaning toilets. Forget the old maxim about nothing succeeding like success: Today, in the executive suite, the all-too-prevalent rule is that nothing succeeds like failure.

Huge severance payments, lavish perks and outsized payments for ho-hum performance often occur because comp committees have become slaves to comparative data. The drill is simple: Three or so directors—not chosen by chance—are bombarded for a few hours before a board meeting with pay statistics that perpetually ratchet upwards. Additionally, the committee is told about new perks that other managers are receiving. In this manner, outlandish "goodies" are showered upon CEOs simply because of a corporate version of the argument we all used when children: "But, Mom, all the other kids have one." When comp committees follow this "logic," yesterday's most egregious excess becomes today's baseline.

In his 2006 letter, Buffett implored large institutional shareholders to use their significant ownership positions to vote to reform CEO compensation:

> Irrational and excessive comp practices will not be materially changed by disclosure or by "independent" comp committee members. . . . Compensation reform will only occur if the largest institutional shareholders—it would only take a few—demand a fresh look at the whole system. The consultants' present drill of deftly selecting "peer" companies to compare with their clients will only perpetuate present excesses.

In his 2007 shareholder letter, Buffett applauded the passage of legislation to require the expensing of stock options. But he wryly noted that only 2 out of 500 large publicly traded companies had chosen to directly expense their stock options. The remaining 498 chose a second option offered by Congress, probably a victory for corporate lobbyists. Companies that chose to grant options at prevailing market prices were exempted from expensing them.

Buffett failed to mention corporate compensation in his 2008 shareholder letter. Maybe he's thrown in the towel. CEOs, corporate directors, regulators, large institutional investors, and legislators have all failed to exercise their fiduciary duties. This dereliction of duty has unfortunately spawned a new species of capitalist—the corporate raider (1980s term) or hedge-fund manager (second millennium term).

Repossession and Ownership

Corporate raiders and hedge-fund managers consider themselves shareholder champions. Indeed, many of them dig more deeply into a business than do institutional investors and analysts. This should come as no surprise. Private equity investors pocket a big percentage of the profits found in these investigations. They also get to pocket overrides and other fees. What's left over goes to the investors whose money supports these investigations.

Recently, an acquaintance who works for an equity hedge fund asked me how Buffett used Berkshire Hathaway's cash in the early days to buy other companies that were not related to the textile business. While my acquaintance picked up on Buffett's "go forth and multiply" strategy (see Chapter 5), he would flunk other Buffett tests. Like a repo agent, a hedge-fund manager takes over a company that is floundering because of inept management and returns it to the legal owners. He skims off the cash and other liquid assets, then fixes up the business for a quick resale. He pockets fees and a share of the profits. Buffett, on the other hand, wants to buy quality companies for life. He wants—he needs—managers to stay on for life and imprint their values throughout the corporate culture.

Personalities versus Principles

Buffett has built Berkshire by attracting owners and managers of businesses who are emotionally attached to their businesses. These owners, like Buffett, are capitalists, not materialists. They work long hours even though most do not have to work at all. In his 2000 shareholder letter, Buffett described the ideal Berkshire manager:

———

We find it meaningful when an owner *cares* about whom he sells to. We like to do business with someone who loves his company, not just the money that a sale will bring him (though we certainly understand why he likes that as well). When this emotional attachment exists, it signals that important qualities will likely be found within the business: honest accounting, pride of product, respect for customers, and a loyal group of associates having a strong sense of direction.

The reverse is apt to be true, also. When an owner auctions off his business, exhibiting a total lack of interest in what follows, you will frequently find that it has been dressed up for sale, particularly when the seller is a "financial owner." And if owners behave with little regard for their business and its people, their conduct will often contaminate attitudes and practices throughout the company.

———

Many such managers mentioned in the first paragraph of the previous quote have been praised in Buffett's shareholder letters: Lou Simpson, the company's chief investment officer; Dave Sokol, the chairman of Berkshire's MidAmerican utilities empire and Buffett's roving business ambassador; Ajit Rain, the mastermind of Berkshire's highly successful reinsurance business; and Charles Huggins and Brad Kinstler of See's Candies. The list goes on and on.

While Buffett brags about the longevity of his managers, other CEOs boast about the people they hire from outside the company. Corporate directors and management expect that this "new blood" will shake up complacent corporate cultures. But this strategy fails when directors confuse personalities with principles. Consider Enron, AIG, and Lehman Brothers—companies where personality-dominant cultures brought on economic collapse. In contrast, Procter & Gamble, Johnson & Johnson, and Berkshire are respected and continue to thrive because they nurture principles-based cultures.

Managers and Meetings

In 2010, a new manager will attend the Berkshire annual meeting for the first time, Matthew Rose, the CEO of

Burlington Northern Santa Fe Railroad. He will sit in a special section with other Berkshire managers not far from where Buffett and Munger answer questions.

Burlington Northern has a long history. Its predecessor company started back in 1870 during America's great railroad expansion. For years, CEO Rose has published shareholder letters that sound a lot like Buffett's. They have consistently ranked among the top-scoring letters in my annual CEO Candor surveys. Rose concluded his 2008 shareholder letter with this story:

As I write this letter, the oldest man in America is a former BNSF employee. His name is Walter Breuning, and he is 112 years old. He dedicated a half century of his life to working for predecessors of BNSF. We are grateful for his years of service. Remarkably, BNSF companies were operating nearly a half century before he was born, and we have continued to operate another half century after his retirement. His story highlights the rich history of BNSF and the United States, as well as the enormous obligation that all of us feel toward protecting the strength, character and continued success of the company.

▬▬

Rose is a leader who understands why Buffett would devote six hours to answering investor questions. The forum-like opportunity for meaningful, not trivial, public discourse is significant. It proves that Buffett upholds the first Berkshire Hathaway principle: "Although our form is corporate, our attitude is partnership."

Woodstock or Camelot:
Ideals, Images, and Greed

*The job of CEOs is now to regain America's trust—
and for the country's sake it's important that they do
so. They will not succeed in this endeavor, however,
by way of fatuous ads, meaningless policy statements,
or structural changes of boards and committees.
Instead, CEOs must embrace stewardship as a way of
life and treat their owners as partners, not patsies.
It's time for CEOs to walk the walk.*

—BERKSHIRE HATHAWAY 2002 SHAREHOLDER LETTER

Buffett calls his annual shareholder weekend the "Wood-stock of Capitalism." It is a compelling but not entirely accurate image. I have yet to see investors strip off their clothes on the exhibition floor or ecstatically dance during the Q&A session. Rather than drop acid, shareholders buy Dairy Queen Dilly Bars to benefit a local hospital. They get their photos snapped with the Fruit of the Loom walking apples and bananas. The drug of choice is chocolate, the See's candies that Buffett and Munger devour throughout the meeting. While Woodstock was a one-time event, Berkshire's meeting has been an annual event for more than four decades. In the early days, however, only a handful of investors traveled to the New Bedford, Massachusetts meeting. In 2008, more than 35,000 investors from six of the seven continents came to the Omaha bash.

What connects these two "happenings"? Both celebrate the building of communities united by shared ideals. At Woodstock, these ideals were free love, peace, and individual expression. At Berkshire, they are uncovering economic value, following the golden rule of partnership, and using common sense.

Images and Ideals

The image of the "Woodstock of Capitalism" is entertaining, but don't confuse it with Buffett's ideals. Daniel

Boorstin in *The Image: A Guide to Pseudo-Events in America* (1961)* explains how these differ:

An image is something we have a claim on. It must serve our purposes. Images are means. If a corporation's image of itself or a man's image of himself is not useful, it is discarded. Another may fit better. The image is made to order, tailored to fit us. An ideal, on the other hand, has a claim on us. It does not serve us; we serve it. If we have trouble striving towards it, we assume the matter is with us, and not with the ideal.

Sure, we could update the image of Berkshire's meeting and compare it to a reality show such as *Capitalist Idol*, or *So You Think You Can Invest*. This would change the entertainment packaging, but it would not alter Buffett's ideals. These old-fashioned virtues—thrift, hard work, fair

*First Vintage Books, 1991.

play, keeping your word, and responsible ownership—don't need updating.

Berkshire versus Teldar Paper

The 1987 movie *Wall Street* introduced a fictional financial icon—the reptilian Gordon Gekko. He is a capitalist *and* a materialist. His success is measured by his possessions. Modeled after headline-making corporate raiders of the time—Ivan Boesky, Michael Milken, and Carl Icahn—Gekko embodies the thrill of winning at any price. He attracted the world's loathing and fascination.

The film's climax takes place at a shareholder meeting in a posh New York City hotel ballroom. Having stealthily accumulated enough shares to become Teldar Paper Company's largest shareholder, Gekko is invited to address his fellow shareholders. He grabs a handheld mike and, in a voice as slick as the gel in his hair, presents himself as a liberator of companies run by inept, caretaking managements that destroy shareholder value. Under the hotel's sparkling chandeliers, he tells Teldar's owners the secret of his success:

The new law of evolution in corporate America seems to be survival of the unfittest. Well, in my book you either do it right or you get eliminated. In the last seven deals that I've been involved with, there were 2.5 million stockholders who have made a pretax profit of 12 billion dollars. Thank you. I am not a destroyer of companies. I am a liberator of them!

The point is, ladies and gentleman, that greed—for lack of a better word—is good. Greed is right. Greed works. Greed clarifies, cuts through, and captures the essence of the evolutionary spirit. Greed, in all of its forms—greed for life, for money, for love, knowledge—has marked the upward surge of mankind.

And greed—you mark my words—will not only save Teldar Paper, but that other malfunctioning corporation called the USA.

Gekko sits down to loud applause. He has won the necessary votes to replace current management. Importantly, he has legitimized greed. In the Gekko dictionary, it is not "an excessive desire to possess more than one needs or deserves." He spins it into a force that will restore America to greatness. Greed is so good that it justifies practically any means to achieve his goals.

In 2010, almost a quarter of a century since *Wall Street* was released, it is impossible to believe that greed will save the United States. Instead, it has led to the greatest global economic collapse since the Great Depression. But something has changed during this time. Unlike the past, when financial collapse was linked to individuals like Boesky, Milken, and Lay and Skilling of Enron, the perpetrators of the 2008 financial collapse are not easily identified. They are our neighbors, the folks we meet at church, and the people whose children play with our own.

The global financial system was ultimately broken by the actions of millions of people who subscribed to the Gekko creed: Don't do what is right, do what is right for you. Consider the mortgage brokers who offered loans that violated the standards of commonsense underwriting, the Wall Street merchandisers who packaged these risky mortgages in AAA-rated securities, and the investors who carelessly bought securities they did not or could not understand. Greed is woven into the fabric of our global in-stitutions—our banks and investing institutions, our gov-erning bodies and communities. A culture of greed justifies institutional agendas that bankrupt the future to pursue short-term personal gains.

Gekko calls the United States a "malfunctioning cor-poration." To him it is no longer a nation founded as a more perfect union to better the lives of the citizens. Instead, it is a corporation whose business is business. When we measure the nation's well-being by the daily ringing of the New York Stock Exchange's closing bell, we can wonder if Gekko was right. But he stumbles when he says, "Greed—for lack of a better word . . ." There are plenty of better words. At a Berkshire Hathaway meeting, for instance, you are more likely to hear the word "stewardship." Imagine this word—describing the actions of a true owner, not a renter—in Gekko's liberation speech:

Stewardship is right. Stewardship works. Stew-ardship clarifies, cuts through, and captures the essence of the evolutionary spirit. Stewardship, in all of its forms—stewardship for life, for money,

for love, knowledge—has marked the upward surge
of mankind.

And stewardship will not only save Teldar Paper, but that other malfunctioning corporation called
the USA.

In Buffett's eyes, corporate raiders like Gekko and care-
taker managers like Teldar's CEO are shirking their stewardship responsibilities. In his 2002 shareholder letter, he
wrote: "Both the ability and fidelity of managers have long
needed monitoring. Indeed, nearly 2,000 years ago, Jesus
Christ addressed this subject, speaking (Luke 16:2) ap-
provingly of 'a certain rich man' who told his manager,
'Give an account of thy stewardship; for thou mayest no
longer be steward.'" Stewards in his vocabulary are managers of businesses that have a duty to care for—not to destroy—what has been entrusted to them.

Buffett's Ovarian Lottery

Lots of people talk about stewardship and making the world
a better place. But Buffett walks his talk. In 2006, he stunned

the world by announcing that he would donate the bulk of his fortune—valued at the time at around $30 billion—to the Bill & Melinda Gates Foundation to help the world's poorest people. My daughter, then 12 years old, wrote him a thank-you letter (with no help from me) that described the importance of his gift:

Dear Mr. Buffett,

Thank you for generously giving money to help people. Wealthy people who have power spend most of their money on luxuries. You don't. For example, people as great as Julius Caesar and Henry VIII became greedy and corrupt. You didn't. I never thought that this would happen to you, and you have proved this.

My Mom wrote a book about how our world could get better. She said that we could stop being greedy and the world would just start to get better. However, I disagree with this. I believe that we have to go through a major breakdown before we can get better. For example, the Great Depression broke down the economy and everything in America. We got better after this. Every country at some point has a "golden age" and then a point where they just break. They have to build themselves up again. This happened in Spain's "golden age" when they discovered the Mayas, Incas, and Aztecs. Next Britain, America, and other cultures had their "golden ages" and breaking points. This must happen to the world again before we can realize our mistakes and correct them for the future. I think that actions like yours can help us to rebuild society.

Buffett leaves his fortune to help others because he never forgets that his success is based on pure chance. He is among only a small fraction of people in the world who are lucky enough to have been born to parents with the means to feed and clothe their children and get them a good education. He pulled a winning ticket in the ovarian lottery because he was born in a country with unique opportunities. He has beaten the odds. His life would have been very different had he been born to parents so impoverished that they could not feed him or even provide clean drinking water. In gratitude for his dumb luck, he offers his fortune so others around the world can have better lives.

Business and Society

Buffett's belief in the ovarian lottery has even influenced his views on taxes. Since he believes that business owes a debt to society, he reports how much Berkshire has paid in taxes—not how much it avoided. In his 1996 shareholder letter, he reminded investors:

Berkshire prospers in America as it would nowhere else. . . In 1961, President Kennedy said that we should ask not what our country can do for us, but rather ask what we can do for our country. Last year we decided to give his suggestion a try—and who says it never hurts to ask? We were told to mail $860 million in income taxes to the U.S. Treasury.

Here's a little perspective on that figure: If an equal amount had been paid by only 2,000 other taxpayers, the government would have had a balanced budget in 1996 without needing a dime of taxes—income or Social Security or what have you—from any other American. Berkshire shareholders can truly say, "I gave at the office."

In his 1998 letter to shareholders, Buffett again reported how Berkshire's shareholders shouldered their tax burden. He tried to rally others to ante up their fair share:

Writing checks to the IRS that include strings of zeros does not bother Charlie or me. Berkshire as a corporation, and we as individuals, have prospered in America as we would have in no other country. Indeed, if we lived in some other part of the world and completely escaped taxes, I'm sure we would be worse off financially (and in many other ways as well). Overall, we feel extraordinarily lucky to have been dealt a hand in life that enables us to write large checks to the government rather than one requiring the government to regularly write checks to us—say, because we are disabled or unemployed.

By 2003, Buffett had bigger fish to fry than goading other companies to pay their fair share. His public criticism of certain Bush administration tax proposals had prompted

Pamela Olson, the assistant secretary for tax policy at the U.S. Treasury, to imply that "a certain Midwestern oracle" was playing the tax code "like a fiddle." Buffett fired back in his shareholder letter:

Alas, my "fiddle playing" will not get me to Carnegie Hall—or even to a high school recital. Berkshire, on your behalf and mine, will send the Treasury $3.3 billion for tax on its 2003 income, a sum equaling 2½% of the total income tax paid by all U.S. corporations in fiscal 2003. (In contrast, Berkshire's market valuation is about 1% of the value of all American corporations.) Our payment will almost certainly place us among our country's top ten taxpayers. Indeed, if only 540 taxpayers paid the amount Berkshire will pay, no other individual or corporation would have to pay anything to Uncle Sam. That's right: 290 million Americans and all other businesses would not have to pay a dime in income, social security, excise or estate taxes to the federal government. (Here's the math: Federal tax receipts, including social security receipts, in fiscal 2003 totaled $1.782 trillion and 540 "Berkshires," each paying $3.3 billion, would deliver the same $1.782 trillion.)

Our federal tax return for 2002 (2003 is not finalized), when we paid $1.75 billion, covered a mere 8,905 pages. As is required, we dutifully filed two copies of this return, creating a pile of paper seven feet tall. At World Headquarters, our small band of 15.8, though exhausted, momentarily flushed with pride: Berkshire, we felt, was surely pulling its share of our country's fiscal load.

But Ms. Olson sees things otherwise. And if that means Charlie and I need to try harder, we are ready to do so.

I do wish, however, that Ms. Olson would give me *some* credit for the progress I've already made. In 1944, I filed my first 1040, reporting my income as a thirteen-year-old newspaper carrier. The return covered three pages. After I claimed the appropriate business deductions, such as $35 for a bicycle, my tax bill was $7. I sent my check to the Treasury and it—without comment—promptly cashed it. We lived in peace.

I can understand why the Treasury is now frustrated with Corporate America and prone to outbursts. But it should look to Congress and the Administration for redress, not to Berkshire.

Corporate income taxes in fiscal 2003 accounted for 7.4% of all federal tax receipts, down from a post-war peak of 32% in 1952. With one exception (1983), last year's percentage is the lowest recorded since data was first published in 1934.

Even so, tax breaks for corporations (and their investors, particularly large ones) were a major part of the Administration's 2002 and 2003 initiatives. If class warfare is being waged in America, my class is clearly winning. Today, many large corporations—run by CEOs whose fiddle-playing talents make your Chairman look like he is all thumbs—pay nothing close to the stated federal tax rate of 35%.

In his 2008 letter to shareholders, Buffett did not boast about paying taxes. Instead, he questioned the irrationality of government policy that for the moment favored financial cripples with government guarantees over companies, like Berkshire, that have played by the rules and built balance sheets as impregnable as the Rock of Gibraltar.

Buffett's 2009 letter does not include references to tax payments. Instead it describes his acquisition of the Burlington Northern Santa Fe Railroad. This company will add as much as $18 billion in revenues and over $2 billion in earnings to Berkshire's income statement. It will position the company for future growth as the American economy recovers and as fuel efficiency becomes a business imperative. CEO Matthew Rose has managed Burlington Northern like a Berkshire owner and will continue to do so. The deal follows Buffett's principles to a "T."

This purchase will change Berkshire in other ways. In order to pay for the railroad, Berkshire shareholders voted to split the Class B class shares on January 20, 2010. This meant that each holder of one share of Class B stock received 50 shares the following day. Instead of trading at over $3,000, each Class B share was valued at about $66. At present, significantly more shares of Class B stock are trading on the market. At a lower price and with more stock available, it is likely that more stock flippers will buy

Berkshire. This may weaken the investor loyalty that Buffett has enjoyed and interfere with his tap dancing.

Buffett turns 80 in 2010. He has lived through many economic cycles. He jokes about his age, but Berkshire watchers may wonder how the company can continue without him. His success shows beyond any doubt that one person can make a whopping difference—but can this last?

Camelot in Omaha

For me, Berkshire has always had the aura of Camelot. The legendary King Arthur had a vision for the world—that righting wrongs, not committing them, was the way to go. He challenged the status quo and forged a community of like-minded knights who put his principles into practice.

Camelot worked for a while—and then it blew up. In the movie *Camelot*, King Arthur's wife, Guinevere, runs off with his best friend, Sir Lancelot. At the end of the film, Arthur is a broken man. It is dawn, and he is preparing to battle Lancelot. He discovers a young boy who has run away from home, eager to fight for the ideals of the Round Table. Not knowing that he is addressing the king, the lad,

Tom of Warwick, tells him stories about the deeds of King Arthur and his knights. His eyes flash with excitement. Gradually, Arthur sees that his ideals are alive in the telling of these tales. He commands the boy to return home and spread his stories of the Round Table. Arthur may not have succeeded in creating a just and law-abiding society, but his example provides a moral standard for future generations.

Buffett's legacy is huge. His example of philanthropy inspires others. His stories of allocating capital for long-term growth offer economically sound standards to monitor CEO performance. His governance of Berkshire shows that partnership principles and common sense can rein in executive privilege and create long-lasting wealth.

We get to choose.

Will we follow the path of stewardship or greed? Will we promote stock ownership or casino capitalism? Will we give our savings to investment managers who buy businesses or who rent stocks? Will we choose the road less taken or continue business as usual? It has been said that one committed person can change the world. Buffett reminds us that the American legacy is built upon the freedom to choose. We get to choose. We *must* choose.

Acknowledgments

Warren Buffett's commitment to words and integrity and his unflinching belief in building economic value remain the gold standard in business. I am grateful to him for setting this standard; and I am equally grateful to him for encouraging me over the years to bring attention to CEO candor. Debbie Bosanek, his hard-charging assistant, has supported the birth of this book from beginning to end. I was also fortunate to get excellent guidance from colleagues John Taylor, Tom Wohlfarth, and Ian Bourne; they are among the smartest corporate finance people I know. Kathleen Cox helped me to see the book as a whole and provided sage commentary when it mattered most; Areta Buk offered valuable creative support. My associate, Stephen Dandrow, spent hours adding informed insights honed by years of analyzing CEO candor in shareholder letters.

I also want to thank my McGraw-Hill editor Mary Glenn, who early on saw this book's potential. She has been an enthusiastic supporter along with Sophia Efthimiatou and Gaya Gayathri. My thanks also go to Ruth Mannino, who never wavered in her commitment to produce a beautiful and informative book. Beth and Phil Black and Diana Abbott of Omaha's Bookworm bookstore were always ready to cheer on *Buffett's Bites* and its earlier cousins. Finally, I want to thank my teenage daughter Lianne, whose candor is nearly always refreshing and who, upon meeting Warren Buffett when she was eight, wisely observed, "He's more of a kid than I am."

TRUST CASH ALWAYS.

THE GOLDEN RULE WORKS IN BUSINESS, TOO.

GREAT LEADERS NEVER UNDERESTIMATE
THE POWER OF WELL-DESERVED PRAISE.

HEALTHY CULTURES CREATE WEALTH;
TOXIC CULTURES DESTROY IT.

TO CREATE LONG-LASTING WEALTH, DON'T LOSE MONEY.

JUDGE CEOS ON THE QUALITY AND
QUANTITY OF THEIR CONFESSIONS.

AIDING INVESTORS' ANALYSIS BUILDS INVESTOR TRUST.

FAILED DISCIPLINE WILL LEAD TO A POORHOUSE,
NOT AN ECONOMIC POWERHOUSE.

REACH OUT IN A CRISIS; DON'T HUNKER DOWN.

A CONCLUSION ABOUT THE ECONOMY DOES NOT TELL US
IF THE STOCK MARKET WILL RISE OR FALL.

GREAT CEOS NEED TO BE
DISCIPLINED CAPITAL ALLOCATORS.

AVOID THE CHICKEN LITTLE SYNDROME.